Critical Prais[e]
TALES OF THE [GONE]

- Winner of a PEN/Beyond Marg[in]
- A *New York Times* Editors' Choic[e]
- An *Essence Magazine* Best Seller

"As this new collection of short fi[ction, some of it previously] unpublished) makes clear, the writer formerly known as LeRoi Jones possesses an outtelligence of a high order. Baraka is such a provocateur, so skilled at prodding his perceived enemies (who are legion) in their tender under-bellies, that it becomes easy to overlook that he is first and foremost a writer . . . He writes crisp, punchy sentences and has a fine ear for dialogue . . . In his prose as in his poetry, Baraka is at his best a lyrical prophet of despair who transfigures his contentious racial and political views into a transcendent, 'outtelligent' clarity."

—NEW YORK TIMES BOOK REVIEW

"A marvelously vital and creative mind at work."

—LIBRARY JOURNAL

"Baraka remains a prodigiously skilled writer. *Tales of the Out & the Gone* is an apt reminder of Baraka's unique ability to touch on politics, race, and identity in a biting vernacular style."

—TIME OUT NEW YORK

"In his signature politically piercing and poetic staccato style, Baraka offers a perspective on social and political changes and a fresh view of the possibilities that language presents in exploring human passions . . . Fans and newcomers alike will appreciate Baraka's breadth of political perspective and passion for storytelling."

—BOOKLIST

"Baraka's ability to load his words with so much artillery results from his understanding of storytelling . . . Th[rough] the resolutions are often delivered like gut-shot punch lines, the circumstances behind the varied plots are complex, and are something too few people take the time to confront."

"Baraka makes his prose jump with word coining—'out-telligent,' 'overstand'—and one-liners . . . The humor and off-the-wall jaunts tackle real issues of race, otherness, and power with pointed irony."

—New York Press

"This literary elder's work, no matter what genre, has never failed to excite, never failed to elucidate and examine the human condition with scathing insight . . . The book's charm lies in its tautness. No words wasted here. *Tales* commands you to pay close attention, lest you miss a great joke or a heartbreaking truth."

—Black Issues Book Review

"Baraka unabashedly steps on toes, but does it in such a way that you close the book thanking him for it. He bends the English language to his liking without stopping to explain himself, which is refreshing from both ideological and technical perspectives."

—Idaho Statesman

"The short fiction here shows controversy is nothing new for the last poet laureate of New Jersey . . . Baraka certainly hasn't gone soft."

—Time Out Chicago

"*Tales of the Out & the Gone* displays Baraka's increasing literary playfulness, intellectual exploration, and passion for intuitive abstract language. The book introduces new readers to Baraka's groundbreaking and ever-changing style."

—Ebony

Lynda Koolish

AMIRI BARAKA (previously known as LeRoi Jones) is the author of numerous books of poetry, fiction, and nonfiction. He was named Poet Laureate of New Jersey by the New Jersey Commission on Humanities, from 2002–2004. His most recent book, *Tales of the Out & the Gone* (Akashic, 2007), was a *New York Times* Editors' Choice and a winner of the 2008 PEN/Beyond Margins Award. He lives in Newark, New Jersey.

HOME

HOME

Social Essays by
**LeRoi Jones
(Amiri Baraka)**

AKASHICLASSICS
NEW YORK

Published by Akashic Books
Originally published in 1966 by William Morrow and Company, Inc.
Copyright © 1961, 1962, 1963, 1964, 1965, 1966, 1971, 2009
    by LeRoi Jones/Amiri Baraka

ISBN-13: 978-1-933354-67-5
Library of Congress Control Number: 2008925938

First Akashic Books printing

Some of the essays in this volume originally appeared in an earlier form
in the following publications:
Cavalier, "American Sexual Reference: Black Male"
Evergreen Review, "Cuba Libre"
Kulchur, "Brief Reflections on Two Hot Shots," "Tokenism,"
    and "Expressive Language"
Liberator, "The Revolutionary Theatre"
Midstream, "What Does Non-Violence Mean?"
The Nation, "In the Ring" (reprinted in this volume under the title
    "The Dempsey-Liston Fight")
Poetry, "A Dark Bag" (a review)
The Saturday Review, "The Myth of a 'Negro Literature'"
New York: The Sunday Herald Tribune Magazine, "LeRoi Jones Talking"

AkashiClassics: Renegade Reprint Series
c/o Akashic Books
PO Box 1456
New York, NY 10009
info@akashicbooks.com
www.akashicbooks.com

These Weights and Measures
for Vashti, Kellie and Lisa,
three twentieth-century foxes.

Table of Contents

2009
HOME (new introduction)   15

1965
HOME (original introduction)   21

1960
Cuba Libre   23

1961
Letter to Jules Feiffer   79

1962
Tokenism: 300 Years for Five Cents   85
"Black" Is a Country   101
City of Harlem   107
Cold, Hurt, and Sorrow (Streets of Despair)   115
Street Protest   118
Soul Food   121
The Myth of a "Negro Literature"   124

1963
Brief Reflections on Two Hot Shots   137
A Dark Bag   142
What Does Nonviolence Mean?   155
The Dempsey-Liston Fight   179
Black Writing   185
Expressive Language   190

1964

Hunting Is Not Those Heads on the Wall   197
LeRoi Jones Talking   204
The Last Days of the American Empire (Including Some Instructions for Black People)   214
The Revolutionary Theatre   236

1965

American Sexual Reference: Black Male   243
Blackhope   263
The Legacy of Malcolm X, and the Coming of the Black Nation   266

STATE/MEANT   281

2009

HOME
(new introduction)

The essays in this book reflect a period of great change and excitement. The title was meant not only to speak of my attempts to analyze and understand what life was like here in the U.S. as the 1950s came to an end and the turbulent '60s swept in, but for me, it was also a conscious attempt to home in on both where I was coming from (literally) and where I was trying to get back to, spiritually and finally, on the very real side.

One heavy and aggravating problem with these early writings is that I've long since changed my views on some topics. There is a neophyte Black Nationalist tag to this book, yet I have been a Marxist since the middle '70s. For instance, the homophobic language in several of the essays, including "American Sexual Reference: Black Male," using the word "fag" homeboy style to refer to the right-leaning liberalism of too many Americans, males as well as females, is wrongheaded and unscientific.

In actuality, the attack was on a social class made comfortable from the super-profits bombed and machine-gunned out of the Third World (and it should be obvious that there has grown a whole sector of Negroes participating in this as well). The sexual reference comes from a ghetto language which used homosexuality as a metaphor for weakness, when in all truth, physically, there were even in my own youthful experience very open homosexuals who could kick most of the straight dudes' behinds. Not to mention the homosexual giants we all have known, who have always been out front sexually and politically. Now I must openly regret and apologize for the use of that metaphorically abusive term that was then part of my vocabulary.

These essays were shaped by the beginning of the Civil Rights movement and surrounding events, including the murder of Emmett Till in Money (you dig?), Mississippi, and the photo of his destroyed face inside *Jet* magazine; Dr. Martin Luther King's marriage to Coretta Scott and their arrival in Montgomery, Alabama; the arrest of Rosa Parks, an experienced activist refusing to sit in the back of a Montgomery bus; the subsequent mobilization and organization of the black community of Montgomery; and the election of Martin Luther King, with his new Ph.D. from Boston University, to the leadership of the Montgomery Improvement Association.

You should understand by now the deep-going sociopolitical jolt such "improvement" made. That was the most incisive cliché of the time, improvement, which meant, minimally, ditching segregation and discrimination, which were among the most frequently used words in the black community as I grew up from the '30s through the '60s.

With the success of the boycott of Montgomery's buses by the unified black community—along with the support they received from other sectors of the city and from around the country as the battle synapsed into a national symbol—many people roared their joy at the triumph. It was an important victory over Afro-American national oppression on the heels of *Brown v. Board of Education* in 1954, the Supreme Court's presumed destruction of segregation in education. (*Separate but Evil* was defeated yet still exists.)

But that victory in Montgomery drove the race freaks to blow up Dr. King's house, and when the news got round the city, masses of black people showed up in front of the destruction, some holding rifles high in the air, calling, "Dr. King, Dr. King, what shall we do?"

He answered something along the lines of, "If any blood be shed, let it be ours!" which propelled him into national leadership via *Time* and *Newsweek* and the double-talking guardians of our standardized Dis. And with this came the open dialectic of the Afro-American national movement, splitting one into two, because my generation—though clearly we had to love and respect Dr. King—rejected that call with our whole-ass selves.

Why? Because Malcolm X had begun to appear, and he said, "Be peaceful, be courteous, obey the law, respect everyone; but if someone puts his hand on you, send him to the cemetery!" There was also a man in the South at the same time, Robert Williams, an ex-Marine in Monroe, North Carolina, who led his new-style NAACP chapter to ambush the Klan and take their hoods and guns. Of course, Uncle Roy Wilkins had Williams removed immediately as NAACP president of Monroe. But the jungle felt the rumble.

At the same time as Monroe and shortly after the Montgomery triumph, Fidel Castro led his army of *barbudos* (bearded ones) into Havana, overthrowing the U.S. mongrel Fulgencio Batista and the Cosa Nostra, so that the idea of revolution was clearly a material force to us. In 1960 I went to Cuba, taking Langston Hughes's place on a delegation of black writers to the country, and witnessed the first anniversary of the Cuban Revolution. (See "Cuba Libre," the first essay in this volume.) My mind and my life were changed forever.

In 1959, Malcolm had appeared for the first time on national TV, Mike Wallace's *The Hate that Hate Produced.* Soon, the Greensboro sit-ins to integrate a nasty Woolworth's helped create the Student Nonviolent Coordinating Committee (SNCC) and the general U.S. student movement. It was SNCC that popularized the Black Panthers, with their creation of the Lowndes County Freedom Organization to register people to vote in Alabama. Malcolm called out "The Ballot or the Bullet," which should still resonate today, after two stolen elections and the Democratic presidential nomination of a colored guy named Obama. From Alabama to Barack Obama, "The Ballot or the Bullet" still makes great sense.

In those years, that bifurcation of the movement— Civil Rights and Black Liberation—reflected the *twoness* of the Afro-American people that Du Bois immortalized in *The Souls of Black Folk* with his analysis of "double-consciousness": to be both black and American. So that we had, in reality, to struggle not only for equal citizenship rights but for self-determination as well.

Self-determination became for us in the North the principal spearhead of our movement motion. And with that, a rising kind of "anti-white" sensibility which deepened with the horrific shock of Malcolm's assassination. So that in 1965, the month after Malcolm's murder, I left Greenwich Village with a small group of black intellectuals and organized the Black Arts Repertory Theatre/School on West 130th Street in Harlem. We announced the opening with a parade of young black artist-activists holding banners and paced by Sun Ra and his Myth Science Arkestra.

The last essay in the book, "The Legacy of Malcolm X, and the Coming of the Black Nation," reflects the fact that those of us who left the Village, and indeed a great number of my generation across the country, were Malcolm's Children. SNCC (when it changed "Nonviolent" in its title to "National"), the Black Arts/Black Theatre Movement, the Black Panther Party, Republic of New Afrika, cultural and revolutionary nationalism—all these were inspired by Malcolm's life and example. As was the last sentence of the original 1965 introduction to this book: "By the time this book appears, I will be even blacker." What I and some of the most thoughtful among us did not yet understand was that "Black" is not an ideology, that the stability of the Black United Front that we sought would encounter Black Nationalists, Black Christians, Black Muslims, Yoruba adherents, black cultural nationalists, black communists, black vegetarians. And some folks who were all of the above.

It was on my return to Newark in 1966 that what I

knew superficially was thrust forcefully upon me to fully understand: that there were classes and class struggle among black people, just like all peoples. Coming home and seeing these struggles around real social and po-litical issues transformed me from cultural nationalist to communist. I had touched some of these bases before, but this was the beginning of struggle on a higher, and perhaps even more fundamental, level.

A luta continua.

Amiri Baraka
Newark, New Jersey
October 2008

1965

HOME
(original introduction)

These essays are placed chronologically (from 1960 to 1965), to show just how my mind and my place in America have changed since the "Cuba Libre" essay.

I have been a lot of places in my time, and done a lot of things. And there is a sense of the Prodigal about my life that begs to be resolved. But one truth anyone reading these pieces ought to get is the sense of movement—the struggle, in myself, to understand where and who I am, and to move with that understanding. (As, for example, the difference in out- and in-look between "The Myth of a 'Negro Literature'" and "Black Writing"; or a liberal piece like "Tokenism: 300 Years for Five Cents" and the changed thinking that evolved into "The Revolutionary Theatre" or "American Sexual Reference: Black Male.") And these moves, most times unconscious (until, maybe, I'd look over something I'd just written and whistle, "Yow, yeh, I'm way over there, huh?"), seem to me to have been always toward the thing I had coming into the world, with no sweat: my blackness.

There were all kinds of roadblocks. Having read all of whitie's books, I wanted to be an authority on them. Having been taught that art was "what white men do," I almost became one, to have a go at it. Having been the only "middle-class" chump running with the Hillside Place bads, I was "saved" from them by my parents' determination and the cool scholarship game which turns stone killers pure alabaster by graduation time. Having been born October 7, my nature was to listen to everybody, to be sensitive to, and look at, everything.

But my tendency, body and mind, is to make it. To get there, from anywhere, going wherever, always. By the time this book appears, I will be even blacker.

1960

cuba libre

Preface

If we live all our lives under lies, it becomes difficult to see *anything* if it does not have anything to do with these lies. If it is, for example, true or, say, honest. The idea that things of this nature continue to exist is not ever brought forward in our minds. If they do, they seem, at their most sympathetic excursion, monstrous untruths. Bigger lies than our own. I am sorry. There are things, elements in the world, that continue to exist, for whatever time, completely liberated from our delusion. They press us also, and we, of course, if we are to preserve the sullen but comfortable vacuum we inhabit, must deny that anyone else could possibly tolerate what we all agree is a hellish world. And for me to point out, assuming I am intrepid enough, or, all right, naïve enough to do so, *i.e.*, that perhaps it is just this miserable subjection to the fantastic (in whatever fashion, sphere, or presence it persists) that makes your/our worlds so hellish, is, I admit, presumption bordering on insanity. But it is certainly true . . . whether I persist or no . . . or whether you believe (at least the words) or continue to stare off into space. It's a bad scene either way.

(*What I Brought to the Revolution*)

A man called me on a Saturday afternoon some months ago and asked if I wanted to go to Cuba with some other Negroes, some of whom were also writers. I had a house full of people that afternoon and since we had all been drinking, it seemed pretty silly for me to suddenly drop the receiver and say, "I'm going to Cuba," so I hesitated for a minute, asking the man just why would we (what seemed to me to be just "a bunch of Negroes") be going. For what purpose? He said, "Oh, I thought that since you were a poet you might like to know what's *really* going on down there." I had never really thought of anything in that particular light. Being an American poet, I suppose, I thought my function was simply to talk about everything as if I knew . . . it had never entered my mind that I might really like to find out for once what was actually happening someplace else in the world.

There were twelve of us scheduled to go to Habana, July 20. Twelve did go, but most were last-minute replacements for those originally named. James Baldwin, John Killens, Alice Childress, Langston Hughes, were four who were replaced. The only other "professional" writer on this trip was Julian Mayfield, the novelist, who went down before the main body with his wife.

At Idlewild airport, the 20th, we straggled in from our various lives, assembling at last at 3 P.M. We met each other, and I suppose, took stock of each other. I know I took stock of them, and was disappointed. First, because there were no other, what I considered, "important" Negro writers. The other reasons were accreted as the trip went on. But what I could get at that initial meeting was: One embarrassingly dull (white) communist, his professional Negro (i.e., unstraightened hair, 1930's bohemian peasant blouses, etc., militant integrationist, etc.) wife who wrote embarrassingly inept social comment-type poems, usually about one or sometimes a group of Negroes being mistreated or suffering in general (usually in Alabama, etc.). Two middle-class young Negro ladies from Philadephia who wrote poems, the nature of which I left largely undetermined. One 1920's "New Negro" type African scholar (one of those terrible examples of what the "Harlem Renaissance" was at its worst). One 1930's type Negro "essayist" who turned out to be marvelously un-lied to. One strange tall man in a straw hat and feathery beard (whom I later got to know as Robert Williams and who later figured very largely in the trip, certainly in my impressions of it). The first Negro to work for the *Philadelphia Inquirer*—I think probably this job has deranged him permanently, because it has made him begin to believe that this (the job) means that white America (i.e., at large) loves him . . . and it is only those "other" kinds of Negroes that they despise and sometimes even lynch. Two (white) secretaries for an organization called The Fair Play For Cuba Committee, who I suppose are as dedicated (to whatever it is they are dedicated to) as they are unattractive. One tall skinny black charming fashion model, who wore some kind of Dior slacks up into the Sierra Maestra mountains (she so reminded me of my sister, with her various younger-generation liberated-type Negro comments, that it made any kind of adulterous behavior on my part impossible). One young Negro abstract expressionist painter, Edward Clarke, whom I had known vaguely before, and grew to know and like very much during this, as he called it, "wild scene." Also at the terminal, but not traveling with us, a tall light-skinned young, as white liberals like to say, "Negro intellectual." It was he, Richard Gibson, who had called me initially and who had pretty much arranged the whole trip. (I understand now that he has just recently been fired from his job at CBS because of his "Cuban activities.")

We didn't get to leave the 20th. Something very strange happened. First, the airline people at the desk (Cubana Airlines) said they had no knowledge of any group excursion of the kind Gibson thought he had arranged. Of course, it was found out that he, Gibson, had letters from various officials, not only verifying the trip, but assuring him that passage, etc., had been arranged and that we only need appear, at 3 P.M., the 20th, and board the plane. After this problem was more or less resolved, these same airline people (ticket sellers, etc.) said that none of our tickets had been paid for, or at least, that the man who must sign for the free tickets had not done so. This man who was supposed to sign the free passes to make them valid was the manager of Cubana Airlines, New York, who, it turned out, was nowhere to be found. Gibson raged and fumed, but nothing happened.

Then, a Señor Molario, the head of the July 26th movement in New York City, appeared (he was supposed to accompany us to Habana), and the problem took on new dimensions. "Of course," Señor Molario said, "there are tickets. I have a letter here signed by the Minister of Tourism himself authorizing this trip. The passes need only be signed by the manager of the New York office of Cubana."

Gibson and the airline people told Molario about the manager's inconvenient disappearance. Molario fumed. Gibson and Molario telephoned frantically, but the manager did not appear. (His secretary said she had "no idea" where he was.) Finally, when it was ascertained that the manager had no intention of showing up by plane time, Señor Molario offered to pay for all our tickets out of his own pocket. Then the other dimension appeared. The two men behind the desk talked to each other and then they said, "I'm very sorry, but the plane is all filled up." Molario and Gibson were struck dumb. The rest of us milled around uncertainly. At 4:30 P.M., the plane took off without us. Five hours later, I suppose, it landed in Habana. We found out soon after it took off that there were thirteen empty seats.

The communist and his wife were convinced that the incident represented an attempt by the U.S. government to discourage us from going to Cuba at all. It seemed a rational enough idea to me.

There was no trouble at all with our tickets, etc., the next day. We took off, as scheduled, at 4:30 P.M. and landed at Jose Martí airport five hours later (8:30 P.M. because of the one-hour time difference). At the airport we were met in the terminal by a costumed Calypso band and a smiling bartender who began to pass out daiquiris behind a quickly set up "Bacardi bar" at an alarming rate. There were also crowds of people standing outside the customs office, regular citizens they looked to be, waving and calling to us through the glass. Between daiquiris, we managed to meet our official interpreter, a small pretty Cuban girl named Olga Finlay. She spoke, of course, better English than most of my companions. (I found out later that she had lived in New York about ten years and that she was the niece of some high official in the revolutionary government.) We also met some people from Casa De Las Americas, the sponsoring organization, as well as its sub-director, a young architect named Alberto Robaina. I met two young Cuban poets, Pablo Armando Fernandez, who had translated one of my poems for *Lunes de Revolución*, the literary supplement of the official newspaper of the revolution, and Guillermo Cabrera Infante, the editor of the supplement.

From the very outset of the trip I was determined not to be "taken." I had cautioned myself against any undue romantic persuasion and had vowed to set myself up as a completely "objective" observer. I wanted nothing to do with the official type tours, etc., I knew would be waiting for us and I had even figured out several ways to get around the country by myself in the event that the official tours got to be too much. Casa De Las Americas, the government, was paying all our bills and I was certain that they would want to make very sure that we saw everything they wanted us to see. I wanted no part of it. I speak Spanish fairly well, can't be mistaken for a "gringo yanqui" under any circumstances, and with the beard and without the seersucker suit I was wearing, I was pretty sure I'd be relatively free to tramp around where I wanted to. So of course with these cloak-and-dagger ideas and amidst all the backslapping, happy crowds (crowds in the U.S. are never "happy". . . . hysterical, murderous, duped, etc., viz. Nathanael West, yes, but under no circumstances "happy." A happy crowd *is* suspect), government-supplied daiquiris, Calypsos, and so forth, I got extremely paranoid. I felt immediately sure that the make was on. (See preface.)

In New York we were told that we would probably be staying at the Hotel Riviera, one of the largest luxury hotels in Habana. However, the cars took us to another hotel, the Hotel Presidente. The Presidente is hardly what could be called a luxury hotel, although I'm sure it was one of the great *tourista* places during the 1930's. Now, in contrast to the thirty-story Hilton and the other newer "jeweled pads" of Habana, the Presidente looked much like the 23rd Street YMCA. It had become, after the advent of the skyscraper hotels, more or less a family residence with about thirty-five permanent guests.

When we got out of the cars and realized that by no stretch of the imagination could we be said to be in a luxury hotel, there was an almost audible souring throughout the little band. The place was fronted, and surrounded, by a wide, raised awning-covered tile terrace. There were rattan chairs and tables scattered all over it. At the top of the stairs, as we entered, a small glass-enclosed sign with movie schedules, menus for the dining room, and pictures of the entertainers who worked (only weekends now) in the hotel bar. There was one working elevator run by a smiling, one-armed, American slang-speaking operator. The sign-in desk was exactly the way they are in movies and I was startled for a moment by the desk clerk, who in his slightly green tinted glasses and thin eyes looked exactly like pictures of Fulgencio Batista.

To further sour our little group, the men were billeted two in a room. Clarke and I managed to get into a room with a connecting door to another room. As soon as we got into our room, the other door opened and the model came through smiling and mildly complaining. She definitely missed the Riviera. However, the three of us established an immediate rapport and I called room service and ordered two bottles before we even took off our jackets.

The liquor was brought upstairs and when I opened the door to let the bellhop in, the essayist and the tall bearded man were standing outside the door also. We invited them in and everyone re-introduced himself. As the evening moved on, and more liquor was consumed, we talked more and more about ourselves. I was most interested in the tall man. His name, Robert Williams, was vaguely familiar. I remembered just where it was, and in what context, I had seen Williams' name. He was the president of the Monroe, North Carolina, branch of the NAACP. He was also the man who had stated publicly that he didn't hold too much with "passive resistance," especially as championed by Rev. Martin Luther King, and he had advocated that the Southern Negro meet violence with violence. He had been immediately suspended by the home office, but the people in his branch had told the New York wheels that if Williams was out so were they. He had been reinstated, but very, very reluctantly. Williams had gone on, as he told us in some detail later, to establish a kind of pocket militia among the Negroes of Monroe, and had managed to so terrorize the white population of the town that he could with some finality *ban* any further meetings of the local Ku Klux Klan. The consensus among the white population was that "Williams was trying to provoke them and they weren't going to be provoked."

Somehow, people in Cuba heard about Williams' one-man war in Monroe and invited him to see for himself what was happening in Cuba. Apparently, when the people who were in charge of trying to attract U.S. Negro tourists to Cuba found out that they drew blanks in their dealings with NAACP people and other "official" Negroes, viz. the tragedy of Joe Louis, they thought Williams would be a good risk. He was. He came down to Habana with Richard Gibson and toured the entire country at government expense, meeting Fidel Castro as well as most of the other important men in the revolutionary government. There were many pictures of Williams in most Cuban newspapers, many interviews given to newspapers and over the various television networks. In most of the interviews Williams put down the present administration of the U.S. very violently for its aberrant foreign policy and its hypocritical attitude on what is called "The Negro Question." He impressed almost all of Cuba with the force of his own personality and the patent hopelessness of official Uncle Sham.

On his return to the States, Williams, of course, was castigated by whatever portion of the American press that would even bother to report that there had been an American Negro "leader" who had actually gone down to Cuba and had, moreover, heartily approved of what he had seen. The NAACP people in New York called Williams in and said he was wasting his talent down in that small town and offered him a good job at the home office in New York. When he was offered a return trip to Cuba, Williams jumped at the chance.

Later in the evening, the two middle-class ladies from Philadelphia turned up, drawn I suppose by all the noise that must have been coming out of our room. The one pretty middle-class lady talked for a while about not being at the Riviera, and what people in Philadelphia had said when she told them she was going to Cuba. I was pretty surprised, in one sense, at her relation of those comments, because the comments themselves, which I suppose must have come from people pretty much like herself, *i.e.*, middle-class, middle-brow young Negroes living in Philadelphia, were almost exactly the same as the comments that had been tossed my way from the various beats, bohemians and intellectuals in Greenwich Village, New York City (of course, given that proper knowing cynicism that is fashionable among my contemporaries). It made me shudder. I mean to find how homogenous most thinking in the U.S. has become, even among the real and/or *soi disant* intellectual. A New York taxicab driver taking me out to Idlewild says . . . "Those rotten commies. You'd better watch yourself, mister, that you don't get shot or something. Those guys are mean." And from a close friend of mine, a young New York poet, "I don't trust guys in uniforms." The latter, of course, being more reprehensible because he is supposed to come up with thought that is alien to the cliché, completely foreign to the well-digested particle of moral engagement. But this is probably the biggest symptom of our moral disintegration (call it, as everyone else is wont, complacency), this so-called rebellion against what is most crass and ugly in our society, but without the slightest thought of, say, any kind of direction or purpose. Certainly, without any knowledge of what could be put up as alternatives. To fight against one kind of dullness with an even more subtle dullness is, I suppose, the highwater mark of social degeneracy. Worse than mere lying.

In 1955, on leave from an airbase in Puerto Rico, I came into Habana for three days. I suppose, then, probably next to Tangiers, Habana was the vice capital of the world. I remember coming out of my hotel and being propositioned by three different people on my way to a bus stop. The first guy, a boy around fifteen, wanted to sell me his sister. The second guy, also around fifteen, had a lot of women he wanted to sell. Probably not all of them were his sisters. The third guy had those wild comic books and promises of blue movies. The town was quieter in the daytime; then it was only an occasional offer to buy narcotics. No one even came out on the streets except billions of beggars and, of course, the Americans, until the sun went down . . . then it was business as usual. The best liberty town in the world. I remember also blowing one hundred bucks in the casino and having some beautiful red-haired women give it back to me to play again. She was the wife of a bigtime British film maker who said she was in love with Africans. She was extremely dragged when she found out I was just an American G.I. without even money enough to buy a box of prophylactics.

(What I Brought Back Here)
The next morning I was awakened by the phone on the night table next to my head. It was the historian, who had assumed the role of official spokesman, etc., and, I suppose, coordinator of the group. He said that the group was waiting for Clarke and me to come down, hadn't we been advised as to what time to meet in the lobby, etc.

Our official guides and interpreters were waiting, Olga Finlay and the architect, Robaina. Robaina, about twenty-eight years old and blond, wore a fairly expensive Italian suit and was driving a white Jaguar. He spoke almost no English, though he understood it perfectly, but had to go along with us because he was sub-director of the sponsoring organization.

That was our first stop, Casa De Las Americas. It was housed in a large white building about three blocks from the Presidente. The organization itself is responsible for disseminating and promoting Cuban culture throughout the Americas. It is also responsible for such things as inter-cultural exchanges between Cuba and other countries: traveling art shows, arranging visits to Cuba by American (North and South) persons from all the arts, setting up writers conferences (such as the one that included Simone de Beauvoir and Jean Paul Sartre), running an adult education center, discussion groups, lecture series, and hundreds of other things. They've had a few North Americans down to lecture and perform: William Warfield gave several concerts all over the country, Waldo Frank lectured, and Maya Deren, the experimental film maker, was down in May, showing her films and lecturing. Many more North American artists, etc., have been invited to come down just to see what's going on in the country, but most have refused or been very busy.

The adult school, which is run very much like the New School for Social Research, specializes in what's known as "Cultura Para El Pueblo" (Culture For The People). The courses of study are French, English, Portuguese, American History, Cuban History, Cuban Literature, Political Geography, Latin-American Literature, Music, North American Literature, and one in Film. The library, which specializes in "Asuntos Americanos," has about 25,000 volumes, including literary magazines from all over the Americas.

La Casa also maintains a record library of Latin-American music, classical as well as folk. They also serve as a publishing house for Latin-American authors, having just conducted this spring an inter-Latin-American competition for the best new books, poetry, drama, short stories, a novel, and a collection of essays. The prizes were $1,000 and publication of the work. Two Argentines, a Cuban, a Guatemalan and an Ecuadorian won the first prizes.

The place is a jumble of activity. Even early in the morning when we got there, there were secretaries running through the various offices speaking Spanish, Portuguese, English and French. We were introduced to the director of La Casa, Señora Haydee Santamaria, a blonde buxom woman of about forty. The first thing she told us, through Olga, was that although special tours had been arranged for our party, we were free to go anywhere we could. This brought a low roar of approval from the group, although the communist and his wife said they hoped the official tour would include at least one peasant's home and a typical Cuban Negro family. Señora Santamaria said that if the tours did not already include these things, she would make sure they were added. She talked to us briefly about La Casa's functions and had small pamphlets passed around which went into these functions in detail. We were also given copies of the five prizewinning books I mentioned before, even though the only members of our party who could read or speak Spanish were the essayist and myself.

The small demitasse cups of Cuban coffee were served and we asked Señora Santamaria questions as well as the other employees of La Casa who were present for just that purpose. Robaina was standing next to me so I began to ask him about Cuban poets. Were there any literary magazines in Cuba? What were the young poets like? What was Cuban painting like? Would I get a chance to meet Nicolas Guillen (the best known Cuban poet—he and Neruda are considered the best living Latin-American poets). Robaina's English conversation was mostly Spanish, but we got on very well. He answered almost all of my questions energetically and even offered to take me around to see some of the young Cuban painters and poets.

We hung around La Casa another hour then went downstairs to the production offices of *Arma Nueva*, the organ of La Comisión Nacional De Alfabetización, the organization in charge of elementary adult education. This organization is attempting to educate the great masses of illiterate Cubans concentrated mostly in rural areas. They number more than two million throughout the country. *Arma Nueva* is "a review for rebel soldiers, workers, and farmers." Most of the articles in the magazine deal with popular heroes, current events and sports and are written the way a child's primer is. In the edition I received, there were articles on Great Cuban Women, Great Cuban Sports Figures, The Seas Around Cuba, What Is a Biography?, The Life of Camilo Cienfuegos, The Agrarian Reform, A History of Cuba in 10 Paragraphs, The Battle of "El Uvero," What Is a Cooperative, The Rebel Army, and many features like crossword puzzles, double crostics, etc. Each article, as well as giving basic information, attempts to point out the great changes in Cuba since the revolution. Each article is, of course, trying to do two things at once, educate as well as proselytize. For example, one of the word games went: "Who is the chief of the Cuban revolution?—FIDEL." "What is the principal product of Cuban economy?—SUGAR." "What is the hope of all the people?—LIBERTY."

These offices were small and in the basement of La Casa. There were about five young men busily stapling mimeographed announcements inside the current issue of *Arma Nueva*. They all got up to shake our hands and greet us when we came in. The only young woman in the office gave us a brief talk about the magazine, and the adult education program in Cuba. Most of the people in the office seemed to recognize Robert Williams immediately, and after the young woman's talk, some of the young men left their stapling to ask Robert about the

U.S. and why he thought U.S. newspapers told so many lies. One of them asked, "Are they paid to lie? Don't they ever tell the truth about what's happening down here? That man in the *Times* [Tad Szulc] is a filthy liar. He should be kicked out of the country and an honest man brought down." Robert thought this was funny and so did I, but I could see the possible headlines in the *New York Times* if said Szulc were to have overheard this exchange. CUBAN EXTREMISTS ADVOCATE EXPULSION OF U.S. NEWSMEN.

We drank some more Cuban coffee and hit the road again.

At the Ministry of Education, a prewar, Spanish style office building in old Habana, we met the assistant minister (or sub-secretary) of education, Doctor José Aguilera. The minister, a short dark man in his forties, talked about an hour, with frequent interruptions, about the educational situation in Cuba. He compared the status of the Cuban educational system as of January 1, 1959, with the system as it stood now; outlining the many changes the revolutionary government has brought about. The statistics were staggering. In their excellent book *Cuba: Anatomy of a Revolution*, Leo Huberman and Paul M. Sweezy give exact facts and figures, comparisons outlining precisely how far, not just the educational system has come since the first days of the revolutionary government, but just how much extreme progress has been made in all areas of economic, social and cultural adjustment. It would seem to me that since the *New York Times* is usually so fond of facts and statistics, it would reprint a few of the innumerable graphs, charts and tables in this book instead of printing long, tiresomely untrue "reports" by middle-class Americans suffering from that uniquely American sickness called "identification." This is a disease wherein the victim somehow thinks that he receives monies or other fringe benefits from Standard Oil, Coca-Cola, Du Pont, U.S. Steel, etc., and feels genuinely hurt if some of "their properties" are expropriated. "They're taking *our* oil and *our* Coca-Cola."

Dr. Aguilera talked softly and convincingly, smoking constantly. The Cuban coffee came in, and he had some pamphlets passed around the table, as well as a few examples of new Cuban schoolbooks. (This had been a country of notoriously few schoolbooks.) He gave us copies of what had been the first first-aid book printed in Cuba for general use, then went on calmly and confidently citing statistics as only a government official can. "In the last seven-year period," he said, "a total of only 400 classrooms were created. The revolutionary government by September 1960 will have created almost 10,000. As Fidel said, we're changing every former Batista military fortification into a school. School cities we call them. You'll probably get a chance to visit a few before you leave. (We did the next day.) To show you the amount of blatant corruption that infested this country before the revolution, the educational budget during the years 1907–08, the beginning of the republic, was $4,208,368. The index of illiterates then was 31.47 per cent. Fifty years later, in 1958–59, the budget was $88,389,450, twenty-two times larger, but the index of illiterates remained the same. Only about 8.9 per cent of people between the ages of twelve and nineteen (secondary school age) received any schooling at all. That meant only about 9 out of 100 young people were receiving any secondary schooling at all."

Most of the ladies in our group gasped politely, genuinely impressed. The minister went on: "Another very, very amusing fact about the Cuban education system is that in 1959, just before the revolutionary government took over, there were 24,011 teachers in Cuba, but 1,514 of them were school inspectors." The minister briefly turned the pages of one of the pamphlets he had given us and then with a broad smile resumed his statistics. "Yes, 1,514 inspectors in this little country. Do you know that in the countries of Belgium and France combined they have only 760 inspectors." Everybody in the office broke up. "Well, we've reduced the number of inspectors to around 400, which still means we've got about 80 more than France, a country whose population is eight times larger than ours."

Robert Williams poked me in the side. "Ol' Fulgencio must have had a bunch of relatives."

The group then began to ask questions of the minister. He answered most of them very thoroughly, sometimes asking the opinions of some of his aides who were in the room. More statistics were cited, photographs of old, now demolished school buildings were shown, photos of the new school city in Oriente, "Camilo Cienfuegos," other new school cities just being built. Then the communist's wife wanted to know if in the new schoolbooks that were being manufactured, little Negro children were portrayed as well as white. The minister did not understand at first, or rather, his interpreter did not. The wife said, "I mean, to show the little Negro children that they are not inferior, I think you should have little colored boys and girls in schoolbooks as well as little white boys and girls." I began to laugh very impolitely, and the woman silenced me with a cold look of dignity. When the interpreter got through explaining to the minister again, the puzzled look did not leave his face, but he picked up a few new geography books and thumbed quickly through them. When he reached the page he wanted, he pressed it down and handed it to the woman. She smiled ecstatically and showed the book to her husband. The minister handed her a newly printed notebook for elementary schools; on the cover were five children at a blackboard, two of them black. The woman almost swooned. The minister laughed and shook his head.

We scrambled into waiting cabs and Olga told us our next stop was The National Agrarian Reform Institute (INRA). The Agrarian Reform Law is the basic law passed by the revolutionary government. And it is the application of this law, and its subsequent repercussions, that have been largely responsible for the shaping of public opinion (i.e., opinions of specific governments and their subsequent popularization throughout the populations controlled by these governments) about the new Cuban government, whether pro or con. The Agrarian Reform Law is radical social legislation. As Fidel Castro himself admitted. "I am a radical," he said, "a very radical young man. But I am right."

The INRA is responsible for seeing that the statutes of the Agrarian Reform Law are carried out. The head of the institute, Dr. Antonio Nuñez Jiménez, is responsible only to Fidel Castro. Once one is in Cuba it becomes more than vaguely apparent that the Agrarian Reform and its continued fulfillment by the new government is the key to their success, and that as long as this law is upheld, the majority of the Cuban people will love Fidel Castro even if it were proven that he was Lucifer himself.

We left Old Habana and passed the huge white monument to Jose Martí, the father of the Cuban republic. The institute is a massive white building still in the last stages of completion. It was begun by Batista for some now obscure purpose, but after the revolution the INRA offices were moved in immediately.

The entire front walk of the glass and stone building was covered with milling crowds. Mostly the crowd was made up of rebel soldiers and *campesinos* (peasant farmers). The *campesinos* had probably come from one of the many rural areas of the country to settle some business affair at the institute. They wear the traditional big straw hats with the front brim turned up and all carry the also traditional machete. As we got out of the cabs, a small unit of *miliciana* marched by. The *miliciana* are the female contingent of the home guard that has been formed all over the island. The various units are usually made up of particular age groups. Some, like the one that was passing us, were made up of teenage girls, others include older women, some even younger girls. This unit wore dark skirts, maroon shirts, and dark berets. They moved by in perfect step; a pretty young red-haired girl stepping beside the main body called out cadence loud and clear.

There were two soldiers sitting just inside the glass doors. They smiled at us as we went by, one pointing over his shoulder toward an information desk. Another soldier sat behind the information desk reading a newspaper, beside him one of the young girl *miliciana*. Olga spoke to the soldier briefly and he waved us on. The elevators were so crowded we had to go up in smaller groups. Everywhere in the building there were young soldiers, many of them bearded, all of them carrying some sort of firearm. There were also hundreds of farmers walking around, some even with their wives, children, and huge lunch pails. The noise in the lobbies was unbelievable.

We went into a quiet air-conditioned office with great windows looking out at the sea. A speaker on one of the walls kept up a steady hum of music as well as news broadcasts and announcements. A very dark Negro welcomed us in Cuban English as did a tall blond man who sounded like an Irishman. We were given chairs, and the Irishman, after talking to Olga, dragged out a huge wooden map of Cuba. Another man came out of an inner office, very tall and thin with a neat Latin mustache. He greeted everyone in the office very warmly. He was about thirty, and wore a loose-fitting Brooks Bros. type suit, with an open-collared button-down shirt. He was one of the directors of one agency of the institute. He spoke very bookish English, but seemed to become embarrassed when he couldn't find proper adjectives so he asked Olga to interpret.

Using the huge map, which showed how the country was divided into provinces, he began to outline INRA's responsibilities and the different problems that confronted it. He too began citing reams of statistics, and the Irish-sounding man joined in. Soon, we were having a joint lecture, neither of the men seeming to get in the other's way. "The reason the Cuban economy and thereby most of the people were in such bad shape," said the Irishman, "is that before the revolution we were a monoculture, most of the cultivated land being given over to the growing of sugar cane. Do you know we even imported rice from the United States. Somebody was paying off. Most of the land was owned by large corporations that employed the Cuban labor force for only three months a year, leaving them to starve in the off season. And most of the people did starve. The average per capita income in 1950–54 was about $312.00 per year. Small farms under twenty-five acres made up only about 3.3 per cent of total land holdings. They were almost nonexistent. The majority of farms in the country were being planted and worked by people who did not own the land: sharecroppers. We were a nation of sharecroppers and squatters. Most of the workable land was in the hands of absentee landlords, in some cases foreign corporations."

The tall man butted in: "That's why The Agrarian Reform Law was so important. That's also why it was so controversial." He went to a desk and picked up copies of a mimeographed booklet, and beckoned for one of the uniformed young men to pass them around to us. "The first article of the law is the basis for our revolution. It is the only thing that makes us a sovereign country." He read it to us. "Article One. Latifundium (uneconomic and extensive production of large land holdings) is hereby proscribed. The maximum area of land that may be possessed by a natural or juridical person shall be thirty *caballerias* (about 1,000 acres). The lands belonging to a natural or juridical person that exceed that limit will be expropriated for distribution among the peasants and agricultural workers who have no land."

This meant of course that United Fruit, American Sugar, etc., got burnt immediately. The tall man went on, "And of course, the direct complement to this basic tenet of the reform law is Article Sixteen. It says that an area of two *caballerias* (about 66 acres) of fertile land, without irrigation and distant from urban centers, is established as the 'vital minimum' for a peasant family of five persons engaged in crops of medium economic yield."

"That *is* communism," one of the ladies next to me said half jokingly.

"Is it wrong?" the tall man wanted to know. The woman agreed that it was not.

After more questions, a soldier came into the office and said a few words to Olga. She stood up and our interview with these young men was over. "We're in luck," she said. "We're going to be able to get in to see Antonio Nuñez Jiménez, the executive director of INRA, for about ten minutes." We all got up, finished our coffee, and began shaking hands with everyone in the office.

Nuñez Jiménez's office was directly across the hall from the office we were leaving. In the outer office, a large, smoothfaced Negro soldier sat at a desk typing. He had a huge pearl-handled .45 strapped to his hip and faultlessly polished boots. When we came in, he spun around in his secretary's chair and let us have all thirty-two teeth. He recognized Robert Williams immediately and shook his hand vigorously. While we sat in the outer office waiting for our interview, Williams enthralled him, at his request, with unbelievable tales about separate toilets and chromatic buses. The soldier was obviously too intelligent to believe all of the stories. He kept saying, "Ah, mon, go on!"

Finally, another soldier, this one carrying what Williams described to me as "a new Belgian automatic rifle," came out of the inner offices and beckoned to Olga. There were two more offices inside the one we had waited in. They were filled with clerical workers and soldiers. The door to Nuñez Jiménez's office was standing open and we all crowded in. There were two other soldiers in the office besides the executive director, both with .45's. There were also two young Negroes in civilian clothes talking to each other very animatedly. When we came through the door, Dr. Jiménez wheeled away from his conversation and made a polite Latin bow with both hands extended in greeting. Everyone shook his hand. After the many handshakes he began talking pleasantly to our interpreter. She conveyed his greetings to the group and then began to laugh as she continued to translate the Captain's words. "Dr. Nuñez says that he is glad there are still Americans who want to see Cuba even though the travel agencies no longer think of it as the paradise just five hours from Manhattan. From a paradise to a hell in little over a year . . . we're making progress no matter how you look at it."

While we laughed, one of the soldiers passed out cigars to the men from a box that was on Dr. Nuñez's desk. Some of the group began to ask questions. The Captain did his best to answer all of them. While he was doing this, the model leaned over to me and whispered, "God, he's beautiful! Why're all these guys so good-looking?"

And she was right, he was beautiful. A tall, scholarly looking man with black hair and full black beard, he talked deliberately but brightly about everything, now and then emphasizing a point by bringing his hands together and wringing them in slow motion, something like college English professors. He wore the uniform of the rebel army with the black and red shoulder insignia of a captain. A black beret was tucked neatly in one of his epaulets. He also carried a big square-handled .45.

Finally one of the secretaries asked, "Dr. Jiménez, why is it everyone, even high-ranking officials like yourself, still carry weapons?" There were embarrassed titters from other people in the group, but I thought it the highwater mark of most of the questioning so far.

The Captain smiled cheerfully and ran the fingers of one hand from his mustache to the tip of his beard with that gesture characteristic of most men with beards. "Well, señorita, we are still a revolutionary government, and as such we are still liable to attack by our enemies. Actual physical attack, not just terrible speeches a thousand miles away. We have to be ready for such developments, and we have to let our enemies know that we're ready."

"But don't you think there's been enough killing," the woman continued.

Nuñez Jiménez stopped smiling for a second and looked down at his shiny-handled weapon. "I've never killed anyone in my life. I was a professor at the University. But it is just because I feel that there's been enough killing that I and the other members of the revolutionary government carry these weapons. We have to carry them until we are strong enough to defend ourselves diplomatically. There are people all over the world who would like for us never to become that strong."

After he had stopped answering questions, the Captain passed out copies of a book he had written that had just been published called *La Liberación De Las Islas*. Most of the group had him autograph their copies; when I filed past I took the book, tucked it under my arm and shook the minister's hand. He said, "No autograph?" I answered in Spanish, telling him that I thought the speech and handshake were fine enough souvenirs. He asked was I an American? and I told him that I was an American poet, which meant that I wasn't a real American like Señor Nixon or Arthur Godfrey but that I had certainly been born in that country. He slapped his sides laughing and shouted my answer to his aides.

The last stop was the Ministry of Housing. We were talked to there by a young man of about twenty-seven in a tattersall vest and desert boots. He was one of the sub-directors of the ministry. He used charts, pamphlets, and scale models of new housing to illustrate his points. He talked earnestly and excitedly for an hour and then we left for the hotel. As we were leaving I didn't see Ed Clarke, so I thought he had gotten separated from the party. I went back upstairs with Robaina, the architect, to try and locate him. We met the sub-director in the elevator and after he had helped us look vainly around the now empty halls for Clarke (he had left earlier), we began to talk about the States where, it turned out, he had lived for about six or seven years. One thing he was extremely interested in was whether Miles Davis, the trumpet player, was playing again and healthy after the terrible beating a policeman had given him outside of a nightclub where Miles was working. I told him that Miles was fine and playing as well as ever. "Wow," the sub-director of housing said, "that place is turning into a real police state."

After dinner, Clarke, the essayist and I went into Old Habana to look around. We walked down almost every narrow street and back alley in that section of the city, peering into cafés, ogling the women, talking to bus drivers, thinking we looked pretty Cuban. The essayist and I spoke Spanish, and Clarke is the kind of light-skinned, straight-haired Negro that looks very Latin. Finally we stopped in one particularly grubby bar in the real 42nd Street part of town.

We went in and I said to the bartender, "Tres cervezas, por favor."

The bartender asked, "Que clase?"

I looked at Ed and said, "Hey, what kind of beer you want?" He told me and the bartender whipped around and got them.

We had barely begun to sip the beer when a large stocky man across the bar, who was drunker than he should have been, raised his head, probably for the first time in three hours, and stared across the bar at us. Then he growled very drunkenly, "Abajo imperialismo Yanqui! Viva Cuba Libre!" Then his head slumped again unwillingly. The three of us on the other side of the bar looked at each other with whatever expression comes into people's faces in that kind of situation and tried to continue sipping calmly. The man raised his head again, "Abajo imperialismo Yanqui! Viva Fidel! Viva Cuba Libre!" His head slumped. Clarke nudged me. The essayist made a face. I looked at my foot. "Cuba Sí, Yanqui No! Cuba Sí, Yanqui No! Venceremos!" (We will win.) The head was up again.

Other people in the bar began to look up at us and smile or happily nudge their friends. This time the essayist called across to the man in Spanish. "Look, friend," he said firmly, "if you're talking to us, there's no need to, we readily agree with you. Down with Yankee imperialism. Cuba Yes, Yankee No! It's true." I tried to find my cigarettes.

The man seemed to gather strength from my companion's intrusion and began to shout even louder, then he began to come around the bar toward us. The essayist repeated what the man had just said and Clarke put the newspaper he'd been carrying on the bar. I turned to face the man, hoping I was smiling. But the man sidestepped me and walked around to the essayist and began to talk very loudly, waving his newspaper, instructing my friend on the spot in the virtues of the Cuban revolution and the evils of American imperialism. The essayist agreed and agreed. Clarke and I were agreeing also, but the man never turned to face us. He went on and on. Finally, the bartender came over and told him to be quiet. He lowered his voice one half-decibel and continued his seemingly endless tirade. I thought the only sensible thing was to get out of the place, so I dumped the rest of the beer down my throat, pointed at Clarke's and tried to step between the loud man and his prey. The prey resisted, shaking his finger in the man's face, stopping only long enough to tell me that he was trying to tell this fellow that not all Americans were John Foster Dulles, and that there were still some intelligent people left in the country. That seemed like a pretty farfetched idea to try to convince a Cuban of, so I ordered another beer and tried to relax. The two men wailed on and on.

Presently a shabbily dressed Negro, who was obviously a drifter, came in the bar with a sketchbook under his arm. He came over to where the discussion was raging, stood for a second, then looked over at Clarke and me. Finally he said to me, "Hey man, you American?" I nodded resignedly. "Yeh, yeh, no kidding?"

"That's right," I mumbled, "but only if you don't want to argue."

"Argue?" He pulled up a stool and sat in front of us. "No, man, I don't argue. You my brother." He pointed at his dark arm and then my own. "I just want you to tell me about Harlem. Tell me about Harlem, man."

This was the wildest thing I'd heard all night. I almost fell off the stool laughing. "What's the matter, didn't you read Jimmy Baldwin's article in *Esquire*?"

"What?" He looked at me quizzically. "Que dice?"

"Oh, forget it." I then proceeded to tell him about Harlem as best I could, not even leaving out Hulan Jack and Adam Clayton Powell. While I told him about Harlem, he drew an awful little sketch of me on the back of a matchbook cover which he titled "The Comic." I also bought him two beers and promised to show him around Harlem if he ever got to the States.

When we got to leave the bar around four in the morning, the essayist and his assailant were still agreeing violently. When we left the bar, the man followed us all the way to the bus stop, promising to show us Habana.

* * *

The next day toward afternoon, we drove out first to a beach club called El Obrero Circulo, one of the hundreds of formerly privately owned beach clubs that have since been expropriated and turned into public resorts. "La Playa es por El Pueblo," a big sign outside the beach house said. (The beach is for the people.) It was a marvelous white beach with unbelievably blue water and hundreds of beautiful women, but true to my American heritage, I sat in the bar and drank daiquiris till it was time to leave.

When we got back to the hotel bar, Ed Clarke between sips of beer asked me, "Hey, have you seen any old people? There's nothing but young people running this country. What is Fidel, thirty-three? Ché, Nuñez Jiménez, both in their early thirties. Raul's not even that old. What'd they do to all those old people?"

I laughed. "They must all be in Miami." But it was true, the wild impression one gets from the country is that it is being run by a group of young radical intellectuals, and the young men of Latin America are *radical*. Whether Marxist or not, it is a social radicalism that they want. No one speaks of compromise. The idea has never occurred to them. The many so-called friends of Castro who have run out since the revolution were in most cases people who were prepared to compromise. People who knew that Fidel's radicalism would make him dangerous to the "free world." That free world of bankers, political pawns, grasping industrialists and liars. The free world that cited the inhumanity of the government of Fulgencio Batista an "internal problem," just as they now condone the hateful willfulness of Generalissimo Trujillo (whose picture, until a few months ago, was plastered up all over Cooper Square in New York City).

The weird stupidity of this situation is that in most cases the so-called American intellectual is not even aware of what is happening any place in the world. Not any place where it serves the interests of the various trusts and gangsters that situations be obfuscated. The intelligent American reads an "account" of what is happening someplace in the world, say in the *New York Times*. He is certainly aware to a certain extent that some of what is being "accounted" is slanted in the general direction of American "well-meaningness." The most severe condemnation of American leaders by the American intellectual is that they are "bumblers," unintelligent but well-meaning clowns. But we do not realize how much of the horrible residue of these paid liars is left in our heads. Who is it in the U.S. that is not afraid of China? Who is it that does not believe that there is such a thing as "the free world"? That West Germany is "freer" than East Germany? That there *are* communist influences in the Cuban government? We reject the blatant, less dangerous lie in favor of the subtle subliminal lie, which is more dangerous because we feel we are taking an intelligent stance, not being had. What do we know about China? Who told you about the communist influences in the Cuban government? How do you know the Indian people love Nehru? We go to Mexico for a vacation. The place is a haven for bearded young men of my generation to go and make their "scene," but not one in a hundred will come back realizing that there are students there getting murdered and beaten because they are protesting against the fraudulent one-party regime that controls the country, which is backed to the hilt by our "well-meaning" government.

It is sad, and there is nothing I can even suggest as an alternative. We've gone too far. There is a certain hopelessness about our attitude that can even be condoned. The environment sickens. The young intellectual living in the United States inhabits an ugly void. He cannot use what is around him, neither can he revolt against it. Revolt against whom? Revolution in this country of "due processes of law" would be literally impossible. Whose side would you be on? The void of being killed by what is in this country and not knowing what is outside of it. Don't tell me about the dead minds of Europe. They stink worse than our own.

It was late at night, and still Habana had not settled down to its usual quiet. Crowds of people were squatting around bus stops, walking down the streets in groups headed for bus stops. Truckloads of militia were headed out of the city. Young men and women with rucksacks and canteens were piling into buses, trucks, and private cars all over the city. There were huge signs all over Habana reading "A La Sierra Con Fidel . . . Julio 26." Thousands of people were leaving Habana for the July 26th celebration at Sierra Maestra all the way at the other end of the island in Oriente province. The celebration was in honor of Fidel Castro's first onslaught against Moncada barracks, July 26, 1953, which marked the beginning of his drive against the Batista government. Whole families were packing up, trying to get to Oriente the best way they could. It was still three days before the celebration and people clogged the roads from Habana all the way to the Eastern province.

The night of our departure for Oriente we arrived at the train station in Habana about 6 P.M. It was almost impossible to move around in the station. *Campesinos*, businessmen, soldiers, *milicianas*, tourists—all were thrashing around trying to make sure they had seats in the various trains. As we came into the station, most of the delegates of a Latin-American Youth Congress were coming in also. There were about nine hundred of them, representing students from almost every country in Latin America. Mexicans, Colombians, Argentines, Venezuelans, Puerto Ricans (with signs reading "For the Liberation of Puerto Rico"), all carrying flags, banners, and wearing the large, ragged straw hat of the *campesino*. We were to go in the same train as the delegates.

As we moved through the crowds toward our train, the students began chanting: "Cuba Sí, Yanqui No . . . Cuba Sí, Yanqui No . . . Cuba Sí, Yanqui No." The crowds in the terminal joined in, soon there was a deafening crazy scream that seemed to burst the roof off the terminal. Cuba Sí, Yanqui No! We raced for the trains.

Once inside the train, a long modern semi-air-conditioned "Silver Meteor," we quickly settled down and I began scribbling illegibly in my notebook. But the Latin Americans came scrambling into the train still chanting furiously and someone handed me a drink of rum. They were yelling "Venceremos, Venceremos, Venceremos, Venceremos." Crowds of soldiers and militia on the platform outside joined in. Everyone was screaming as the train began to pull away.

The young militia people soon came trotting through the coaches asking everyone to sit down for a few seconds so they could be counted. The delegates got to their seats and in my coach everyone began to sing a song like "Two, four, six, eight, who do we appreciate . . . Fidel, Fidel, Fidel!!" Then they did Ché (Guevara), Raul, President Dorticos, etc. It was about 1,000 kilometers to Oriente and we had just started.

Young soldiers passed out ham sandwiches and Maltina, a thick syrupy sweet beverage that only made me thirstier. Everyone in the train seemed to be talking excitedly and having a wild time. We were about an hour outside Habana and I was alternating between taking notes and reading about ancient Mexican religion when Olga Finlay came up to my seat accompanied by a young woman. "I told her you were an American poet," Olga said, "and she wanted to meet you." I rose quickly and extended my hand, for some reason embarrassed as hell. Olga said, "Señora Betancourt, Señor LeRoi Jones." She was very short, very blonde and very pretty, and had a weird accent that never ceased to fascinate me. For about thirty minutes we stood in the middle aisle talking to each other. She was a Mexican delegate to the Youth Congress, a graduate student in Economics at one of the universities, the wife of an economist, and a mother. Finally, I offered her the seat next to mine at the window. She sat, and we talked almost continuously throughout the fourteen-hour ride.

She questioned me endlessly about American life, American politics, American youth—although I was jokingly cautioned against using the word *American* to mean the U.S. or North America. "Everyone in this car is American," she said. "You from the North, we from the South." I explained as best I could about the Eisenhowers, the Nixons, the Du Ponts, but she made even my condemnations seem mild. "Everyone in the world," she said, with her finger, "has to be communist or anti-communist. And if they're anti-communist, no matter what kind of foul person they are, you people accept them as your allies. Do you really think that hopeless little island in the middle of the sea is China? That is irrational. You people are irrational!"

I tried to defend myself, "Look, why jump on me? I understand what you're saying. I'm in complete agreement with you. I'm a poet . . . what can I do? I write, that's all, I'm not even interested in politics."

She jumped on me with both feet as did a group of Mexican poets later in Habana. She called me a "cowardly bourgeois individualist." The poets, or at least one young wild-eyed Mexican poet, Jaime Shelley, almost left me in tears, stomping his foot on the floor, screaming: "You want to cultivate your soul? In that ugliness you live in, you want to cultivate your soul? Well, we've got millions of starving people to feed, and that moves me enough to make poems out of."

Around 10 P.M. the train pulled into the town of Matanzas. We had our blinds drawn, but the militia came running through the car telling us to raise them. When I raised the blind I was almost startled out of my wits. There were about 1,500 people in the train station and surrounding it, yelling their lungs out. We pulled up the windows. People were all over. They ran back and forth along the train screaming at us. The Mexicans in the train had a big sign painted on a bedspread that read "Mexico is with Fidel. Venceremos." When they raised it to the windows young men leaped in the air, and women blew kisses. There was a uniformed marching band trying to be heard above the crowd, but I could barely hear them. When I poked my head out of the window to wave at the crowds, two young Negro women giggled violently at first, then one of them ran over to the train and kissed me as hard as she could manage. The only thing to do I could think of was to say "Thank you." She danced up and down and clapped her hands and shouted to her friend, "Un americano, un americano." I bowed my head graciously.

What was it, a circus? That wild mad crowd. Social ideas? Could there be that much excitement generated through all the people? Damn, that people still *can* move. Not us, but people. It's gone out of us forever. "Cuba Sí, Yanqui No," I called at the girls as the train edged away.

We stopped later in the town of Colon. There again the same mobs of cheering people. Camagüey. Santa Clara. At each town, the chanting crowds. The unbelievable joy and excitement. The same idea, and people made beautiful because of it. People moving, being moved. I was ecstatic and frightened. Something I had never seen before, exploding all around me.

The train rocked wildly across and into the interior. The delegates were singing a "cha cha" with words changed to something like "Fidel, Fidel, cha cha cha, Ché Ché, cha cha cha, Abajo Imperialismo Yanqui, cha cha cha."

Some American students whom I hadn't seen earlier ran back and forth in the coaches singing "We cannot be moved." The young folk-song politicians in blue jeans and pigtails.

About two o'clock in the morning they shut the lights off in most of the coaches, and everybody went to sleep. I slept for only an hour or so and woke up just in time to see the red sun come up and the first early people come out of their small grass-roofed shacks beside the railroad tracks, and wave sleepily at the speeding train. I pressed my face against the window and waved back.

The folk singing and war cries had just begun again in earnest when we reached the town of Yara, a small town in Oriente province, the last stop on the line. At once we unloaded from the train, leaving most luggage and whatever was considered superfluous. The dirt streets of the town were jammed with people. Probably everyone in town had come to meet the train. The entire town was decorated with some kind of silver Christmas tree tinsel and streamers. Trees, bushes, houses, children, all draped in the same silver holiday tinsel. Tiny girls in brown uniforms and red berets greeted us with armfuls of flowers. Photographers were running amok through the crowd, including an American newsreel cameraman who kept following Robert Williams. I told Robert that he ought to put his big straw hat in front of his face American ganster style.

From the high hill of the train station it was possible to see a road running right through Yara. Every conceivable kind of bus, truck, car, and scooter was being pushed toward the Sierra, which was now plainly visible in the distance. Some of the *campesinos* were on horses, dodging in and out of the sluggish traffic, screaming at the top of their lungs.

The sun had already gotten straight up over our heads and was burning down viciously. The big straw *campesino* hats helped a little but I could tell that it was going to be an obscenely hot day. We stood around for a while until everyone had gotten off our train, and then some of the militia people waved at us to follow them. We walked completely out of the town of Yara in about two minutes. We walked until we came to more railroad tracks; a short spur leading off in the direction of Sierra Maestra. Sitting on the tracks were about ten empty open cattle cars. There were audible groans from the American contingent. The cars themselves looked like movable jails. Huge thick bars around the sides. We joked about the American cameraman taking a picture of them with us behind the bars and using it as a *Life* magazine cover. They would caption it "Americans in Cuba."

At a word from the militia we scrambled up through the bars, into the scalding cars. The metal parts of the car were burning hot, probably from sitting out in the sun all day. It was weird seeing hundreds of people up and down the tracks climbing up into the cattle cars by whatever method they could manage. We had been told in Habana that this was going to be a rough trip and that we ought to dress accordingly. Heavy shoes, old clothes, a minimum of equipment. The women were told specifically to wear slacks and flat shoes because it would be difficult to walk up a mountain in a sheath dress and heels. However, one of the American women, the pretty young middle-class lady from Philadelphia, showed up in a flare skirt and "Cuban" heels. Two of the Cubans had to pull and tug to get her into the car, which still definitely had the smell of cows. She slumped in a corner and began furiously mopping her brow.

I sat down on the floor and tried to scribble in my notebook, but it was difficult because everyone was jammed in very tight. Finally, the train jerked to a start, and everyone in all the cars let out a wild yell. The delegates began chanting again. Waving at all the people along the road, and all the dark barefoot families standing in front of their grass-topped huts calling to us. The road, which ran along parallel to the train, was packed full of traffic, barely moving. Men sat on the running boards of their cars when the traffic came to a complete halt, and drank water from their canteens. The train was going about five miles an hour and the *campesinos* raced by on their plow horses jeering, swinging their big hats. The sun and the hot metal car were almost unbearable. The delegates shouted at the trucks, "Cuba Sí, Yanqui No," and then began their "Viva" shouts. After one of the "Vivas," I yelled, "Viva Calle Cuarenta y dos" (42nd Street), "Viva Symphony Sid," "Viva Cinco Punto" (Five Spot), "Viva Turhan Bey." I guess it was the heat. It was a long slow ride in the boiling cars.

The cattle cars stopped after an hour or so at some kind of junction. All kinds of other coaches were pulled up and resting on various spurs. People milled about everywhere. But it was the end of any tracks going further toward Sierra. We stood around and drank warm water too fast.

Now we got into trucks. Some with nailed-in bus

seats, some with straw roofs, others with just plain truck floors. It was a wild scramble for seats. The militia people and the soldiers did their best to indicate which trucks were for whom, but people staggered into the closest vehicle at hand. Ed Clarke and I ran and leaped up into a truck with leather bus seats in the back. The leather was too hot to sit on for a while so I put my handkerchief on the seat and sat forward. A woman was trying to get up into the truck, but not very successfully, so I leaned over the rail and pulled her up and in. The face was recognizable immediately, but I had to sit back on the hot seat before I remembered it was Françoise Sagan. I turned to say something to her, but some men were already helping her back down to the ground. She rode up front in the truck's cab with a young lady companion, and her manager on the running board, clinging to the door.

The trucks reared out onto the already heavily traveled road. It was an unbelievable scene. Not only all the weird trucks and buses but thousands of people walking along the road. Some had walked from places as far away as Matanzas. Whole detachments of militia were marching, route step, but carrying rifles or .45's. Women carrying children on their shoulders. One group of militia with blue shirts, green pants, pistols and knives, was carrying paper fans, which they ripped back and forth almost in unison with their step. There were huge trucks full of oranges parked along the road with lines of people circling them. People were sitting along the edge of the road eating their lunches. Everyone going *a la* Sierra.

Our trucks sped along on the outside of the main

body of traffic, still having to stop occasionally when there was some hopeless roadblock. The sun, for all our hats, was baking our heads. Sweat poured in my dry mouth. None of us Americans had brought canteens and there was no water to be had while we were racing along the road. I tried several times to get some oranges, but never managed. The truck would always start up again when we came close to an orange vendor.

There was a sign on one of the wood shack "stores" we passed that read "Niños No Gustan Los Chicle Ni Los Cigarros Americanos Ni El Rocan Rool." It was signed "Fondin." The traffic bogged down right in front of the store so several French photographers leaped off the truck and raced for the orange stand. Only one fellow managed to make it back to our truck with a hat full of oranges. The others had to turn and run back empty handed as the truck pulled away. Sagan's manager, who had strapped himself on the running board with a leather belt, almost broke his head when the truck hit a bump and the belt snapped and sent him sprawling into the road. Another one of the correspondents suddenly became violently ill and tried to shove his head between the rough wooden slats at the side of the truck; he didn't quite make it, and everyone in the truck suffered.

After two hours we reached a wide, slow, muddy river. There was only one narrow cement bridge cross- ing it, so the trucks had to wait until they could ease back into the regular line of traffic. There were hundreds of people wading across the river. A woman splashed in with her child on her shoulders, hanging around her neck, her lunch pail in one hand, a pair of blue canvas sneakers in the other. One group of militia marched right into the brown water, holding their rifles high above their heads. When our truck got on the bridge directly over the water, one of the Cuban newspapermen leaped out of the truck down ten feet into the water. People in the trucks would jump right over the side, sometimes pausing to take off their shoes. Most went in shoes and all.

Now we began to wind up the narrow mountain road for the first time. All our progress since Yara had been upgrade, but this was the first time it was clearly discernible that we were going up a mountain. It took another hour to reach the top. It was afternoon now and already long lines of people were headed back down the mountain. But it was a narrow line compared to the thousands of people who were scrambling up just behind us. From one point where we stopped just before reaching the top it was possible to look down the side of the long hill and see swarms of people all the way down past the river seeming now to inch along in effortless pantomime.

The trucks stopped among a jumble of rocks and sand not quite at the top of the last grade. (For the last twenty minutes of our climb we actually had to wind in and out among groups of people. The only people who seemed to race along without any thought of the traffic were the *campesinos* on their broken-down mounts.) Now everyone began jumping down off the trucks and trying to re-form into their respective groups. It seemed almost impossible. Detachments of *campesino* militia (work shirts, blue jeans, straw hats and machetes) marched up behind us. *Milicianas* of about twelve and thirteen separated our contingent, then herds of uniformed, trotting boys of about seven. "Hup, hup, hup, hup," one little boy was calling in vain as he ran behind the rest of his group. One of the girls called out "Hup, hup, hup, hup," keeping her group more orderly. Rebel soldiers wandered around everywhere, some with long, full beards, others with long, wavy black hair pulled under their blue berets or square-topped khaki caps, most of them young men in their twenties or teenagers. An old man with a full gray beard covering most of his face, except his sparkling blue eyes and the heavy black cigar stuck out of the side of his mouth, directed the comings and goings up and down this side of the mountain. He wore a huge red- and black-handled revolver and had a hunting knife sewn to his boot. Suddenly it seemed that I was lost in a sea of uniforms, and I couldn't see anyone I had come up the mountain with. I sat down on a rock until most of the uniforms passed. Then I could see Olga about fifty yards away waving her arms at her lost charges.

There was a public address system booming full blast from what seemed the top of the hill. The voice (Celia Sanchez, Fidel's secretary) was announcing various groups that were passing in review. When we got to the top of the rise, we could see a large, austere platform covered with all kinds of people, and at the front of the platform a raised section with a dais where the speakers were. Señora Sanchez was announcing one corps of militia and they marched out of the crowd and stopped before the platform. The crowd cheered and cheered. The militia was commended from the platform and then they marched off into the crowd at the other side. Other groups marched past. Young women, teenage girls, elderly *campesinos*, each with their own militia detachment, each to be commended. This had been going on since morning. Hundreds of commendations, thousands of people to be commended. Also, since morning, the officials had been reading off lists of names of *campesinos* who were to receive land under the Agrarian Reform Law. When they read the name of some farmer close enough to the mountain to hear it, he would leap straight up in the air and, no matter how far away from the platform he was, would go barreling and leaping toward the speaker. The crowd delighted in this and would begin chanting "Viva Fidel, Viva Fidel, Viva Reforma Agraria." All this had been going on since morning and it was now late afternoon.

After we walked past the dais, introduced to the screaming crowd as "intellectual North American visitors," we doubled back and went up onto the platform itself. It was even hotter up there. By now all I could think about was the sun; it was burning straight down and had been since early morning. I tugged the straw hat down over my eyes and trudged up onto the platform. The platform itself in back of the dais was almost overflowing, mostly with rebel soldiers and young militia troops. But there were all kinds of visitors also, the Latin American delegates, newsmen, European writers, American intellectuals, as well as Cuban officials. When we got up on the platform, Olga led us immediately over to the speakers' dais and the little group of seats around it. We were going to be introduced to all the major speakers.

The first person to turn around and greet us was a tall, thin, bearded Negro in a rebel uniform bearing the shoulder markings of a *Commandante*. I recognized his face from the papers as that of Juan Almeida, chief of the rebel army, a man almost unknown in the United States. He grinned and shook our hands and talked in a swift combination of Spanish and English, joking constantly about conditions in the United States. In the middle of one of his jokes he leaned backward, leaning over one man to tap another taller man on the shoulder. Fidel Castro leaned back in his seat, then got up smiling and came over to where we were standing. He began shaking hands with everybody in the group, as well as the many other visitors who moved in at the opportunity. There were so many people on the platform in what seemed like complete disorder that I wondered how wise it was as far as security was concerned. It seemed awfully dangerous for the Prime Minister to be walking around so casually, almost having to thread his way through the surging crowd. Almost immediately, I shoved my hand toward his face and then grasped his hand. He greeted me warmly, asking through the interpreter where I was from and what I did. When I told him I was a New York poet, he seemed extremely amused and asked me what the government thought about my trip. I shrugged my shoulders and asked him what did he intend to do with this revolution.

We both laughed at the question because it was almost like a reflex action on my part: something that came out so quick that I was almost unaware of it. He twisted the cigar in his mouth and grinned, smoothing the strangely grown beard on his cheeks. "That *is* a poet's question," he said, "and the only poet's answer I can give you is that I will do what I think is right, what I think the people want. That's the best I can hope for, don't you think?"

I nodded, already about to shoot out another question, I didn't know how long I'd have. Certainly this was the most animated I'd been during the entire trip. "Uh—" I tried to smile—"what do you think the United States will do about Cuba ultimately?" The question seemed weird and out of place because everyone else was just trying to shake his hand.

"Ha, well, that's extremely difficult to say, your government is getting famous for its improvisation in foreign affairs. I suppose it depends on who is running the government. If the Democrats win it may get better. More Republicans . . . I suppose more trouble. I cannot say, except that I really do not care what they do as long as they do not try to interfere with the running of this country."

Suddenly the idea of a security lapse didn't seem so pressing. I had turned my head at a weird angle and looked up at the top of the platform. There was a soldier at each side of the back wall of the platform, about ten feet off the ground, each one with a machine gun on a tripod. I asked another question. "What about communism? How big a part does that play in the government?"

"I've said a hundred times that I'm not a communist. But I am certainly not an anti-communist. The United States likes anti-communists, especially so close to their mainland. I said also a hundred times that I consider myself a humanist. A radical humanist. The only way that anything can ever be accomplished in a country like Cuba is radically. The old has been here so long that the new must make radical changes in order to function at all."

So many people had crowded around us now that it became almost impossible to hear what Fidel was saying. I had shouted the last question. The young fashion model brushed by me and said how much she had enjoyed her stay in Cuba. Fidel touched his hand to the wide *campesino* hat he was wearing, then pumped her hand up and down. One of the Latin-American girls leaned forward suddenly and kissed him on the cheek. Everyone milled around the tall young Cuban, asking questions, shaking his hand, taking pictures, getting autographs (an American girl with pigtails and blue jeans) and, I suppose, committing everything he said to memory. The crowd was getting too large, I touched his arm, waved, and walked toward the back of the platform.

I hadn't had any water since early morning, and the heat and the excitement made my mouth dry and hard. There were no water fountains in sight. Most of the masses of Cubans had canteens or vacuum bottles, but someone had forgotten to tell the Americans (North and South) that there'd be no water. Also, there was no shade at all on the platform. I walked around behind it and squatted in a small booth with a tiny tin roof. It had formerly been a soda stand, but because the soda was free, the supply had given out rapidly and the stand had closed. I sat in the few inches of shade with my head in my hands, trying to cool off. Some Venezuelans came by and asked to sit in the shade next to me. I said it was all right and they offered me the first cup of water I'd had in about five hours. They had a whole chicken also, but I didn't think I'd be able to stand the luxury.

There were more speakers, including a little boy from one of the youngest militia units, but I heard them all over the public address system. I was too beat and thirsty to move. Later Ed Clarke and I went around hunting for water and finally managed to find a small brown stream where the soldiers were filling up their canteens. I drank two Coca-Cola bottles full, and when I got back to Habana came down with a fearful case of dysentery.

Suddenly there was an insane, deafening roar from the crowd. I met the girl economist as I dragged out of the booth and she tried to get me to go back on the front platform. Fidel was about to speak. I left her and jumped off the platform and trotted up a small rise to the left. The roar lasted about ten minutes, and as I got settled on the side of the hill Fidel began to speak.

He is an amazing speaker, knowing probably instinctively all the laws of dynamics and elocution. The speech began slowly and haltingly, each syllable being pronounced with equal stress, as if he were reading a poem. He was standing with the *campesino* hat pushed back slightly off his forehead, both hands on the lectern. As he made his points, one of the hands would slide off the lectern and drop to his side, his voice becoming tighter and less warm. When the speech was really on its way, he dropped both hands from the lectern, putting one behind his back like a church usher, gesturing with the other. By now he would be rocking from side to side, pointing his finger at the crowd, at the sky, at his own chest. Sometimes he seemed to lean to the side and talk to his own ministers there on the platform with him and then wheel toward the crowd calling for them to support him. At one point in the speech the crowd interrupted for about twenty minutes, crying, "Venceremos, venceremos, venceremos, venceremos, venceremos, venceremos, venceremos, venceremos." The entire crowd,

60 or 70,000 people all chanting in unison. Fidel stepped away from the lectern grinning, talking to his aides. He quieted the crowd with a wave of his arms and began again. At first softly, with the syllables drawn out and precisely enunciated, then tightening his voice and going into an almost musical rearrangement of his speech. He condemned Eisenhower, Nixon, the South, the Monroe Doctrine, the Platt Amendment, and Fulgencio Batista in one long, unbelievable sentence. The crowd interrupted again, "Fidel, Fidel, Fidel, Fidel, Fidel, Fidel, Fidel, Fidel, Fidel, Fidel, Fidel, Fidel." He leaned away from the lectern, grinning at the chief of the army. The speech lasted almost two and a half hours, being interrupted time and again by the exultant crowd and once by five minutes of rain. When it began to rain, Almeida draped a rain jacket around Fidel's shoulders, and he re-lit his cigar. When the speech ended, the crowd went out of its head, roaring for almost forty-five minutes.

When the speech was over, I made a fast move for the platform. Almost a thousand other people had the same idea. I managed to shout something to Castro as he was being whizzed to the back of the platform and into a car. I shouted, "A fine speech, a tremendous speech."

He shouted back, "I hope you take it home with you," and disappeared in a host of bearded uniforms.

We were told at first that we would be able to leave the mountain in about three hours. But it had gotten dark already, and I didn't really fancy shooting down that mountain road with the same exuberance with which we came . . . not in the dark. Clarke and I went out looking for more water and walked almost a mile before we came to a big pavilion where soft drinks and sandwiches were being served. The soft drinks were hot and the sandwiches took too long to get. We came back and lay down at the top of a hill in back of the speakers' platform. It drizzled a little bit and the ground was patently uncomfortable. I tried to go to sleep but was awakened in a few minutes by explosions. The whole sky was lit up. Green, red, bright orange: the soldiers were shooting off fireworks. The platform was bathed in the light from the explosions and, suddenly, floodlights from the rear. The public address system announced that we were going to have a show.

The show was a strange mixture of pop culture and mainstream highbrow *haute culture*. There was a choral group singing a mildly atonal tone poem, a Jerome Robbinsesque ballet about Hollywood, Calypso dancers, and Mexican singers and dancers. The last act was the best, a Mardi Gras scene involving about a hundred West Indian singers and dancers, complete with floats, huge papier-mâché figures, drummers, and masks. The West Indians walked through the audience shouting and dancing, their many torches shooting shadows against the mountains. When they danced off and out of the amphitheatre area up toward a group of unfinished school buildings, except for the huge floodlights on stage, the whole area was dark.

Now there was great confusion in the audience. Most Cubans were still going to try to get home that night, so they were getting themselves together, rounding up wives and children, trying to find some kind of transportation off the mountain. There were still whole units of militia piling into trucks or walking off down the hill in the dark. The delegates, our group and a couple more thousand people who didn't feel like charging off into the dark were left. Olga got all the Americans together and we lined up for what was really our first meal of the day: beans, rice, pork, and a small can of fruit juice. At that time, we still had some hopes of leaving that night, but soon word was passed around that we weren't leaving, and it was best that we slept where we were. "Sleep wherever you want," was what Olga said. That meant the ground, or maybe cement sidewalks around the unfinished school buildings and dormitories of the new "school city." Some of the Americans started grumbling, but there was nothing that could be done. Two of our number were missing because of the day's festivities: the young lady from Philadelphia had to be driven back to Habana in a station wagon because she had come down with diarrhea and a fever, and the model had walked around without her hat too often and had gotten a slight case of sunstroke. She was resting up in the medical shack now, and I began to envy her her small canvas cot.

It was a very strange scene, about three or four thousand people wandering around in semi-darkness among a group of unfinished buildings, looking for places to sleep. The whole top of the mountain alive with flashlights, cigarette lighters, and small torches. Little groups of people huddled together against the sides of buildings or stretched out under new "street lamps" in temporary plazas. Some people managed to climb through the windows of the new buildings and sleep on dirt floors, some

slept under long aluminum trucks used for hauling stage
equipment and some, like myself and the young female
economist, sat up all night under dim lights, finally talking ourselves excitedly to sleep in the cool gray of early
morning. I lay straight back on the cement "sidewalk"
and slept without moving, until the sun began to burn
my face.

We had been told the night before to be ready by
6 A.M. to pull out, but when morning came we loitered
around again till about eight o'clock, when we had to
line up for a breakfast of hot milk and French bread. It
was served by young militia women, one of whom wore
a big sidearm in a shoulder holster. By now, the dysentery was beginning to play havoc with my stomach, and
the only toilet was a heavy thicket out behind the amphitheatre. I made it once, having to destroy a copy of a
newspaper with my picture in it.

By nine no trucks had arrived, and with the sun now
beginning to move heavily over us, the crowds shifted
into the few shady areas remaining. It looked almost as
if there were as many people still up on the mountain
as there had been when we first arrived. Most of the
Cubans, aside from the soldiers, stood in front of the pavilion and drank luke-warm Maltina or pineapple soda.
The delegates and the other visitors squatted against
buildings, talking and smoking. A French correspondent
made a bad joke about Mussolini keeping the trains running on time, and a young Chinese student asked him
why he wasn't in Algeria killing rebels.

The trucks did arrive, but there were only enough of
them to take the women out. In a few minutes the sides
of the trucks were almost bursting, so many females had

stuffed inside. And they looked terribly uncomfortable, especially the ones stuck in the center who couldn't move an inch either way. An American newspaper-man with our group who was just about to overstay his company-sanctioned leave began to panic, saying that the trucks wouldn't be back until the next day. But only a half-hour after the ladies pulled out, more trucks came and began taking the men out. Clarke, Williams, another member of our group, and I sat under the tin roof of an unfinished school building drinking warm soda, waiting until the last truck came, hoping it would be the least crowded. When we did climb up into one of the trucks it was jammed anyway, but we felt it was time to move.

This time we all had to stand up, except for a young *miliciano* who was squatting on a case of warm soda. I was in the center of the crowd and had nothing to hold on to but my companions. Every time the truck would stop short, which it did every few yards we traveled, everyone in the truck was slung against everyone else. When the truck did move, however, it literally zoomed down the side of the mountain. But then we would stop again, and all of us felt we would suffocate being mashed so tightly together, and from all the dust the trucks in front of us kicked up. The road now seemed like The Exodus. Exactly the same as the day before, only headed the opposite way. The trucks, the people on foot, the families, the militias, the *campesinos*, all headed down the mountain.

The truck sat one place twenty minutes without moving, and then when it did move it only edged up a few yards. Finally the driver pulled out of the main body of traffic and honking his horn continuously, drove down the opposite side of the road. When the soldiers directing traffic managed to flag him down, he told them that we were important visitors who had to make a train in Yara. The truck zoomed off again, rocking back and forth and up and down, throwing its riders at times almost out the back gate.

After a couple of miles, about five Mexicans got off the truck and got into another truck headed for Santiago. This made the rest of the ride easier. The *miliciano* began opening the soda and passing it around. We were really living it up. The delegates' spirits came back and they started their chanting and waving. When we got to the train junction, the cattle cars were sitting, but completely filled with soldiers and farmers. We didn't even stop, the driver gunned the thing as fast as it would go and we sailed by the shouting soldiers. We had only a few more stops before we got to Yara, jumped down in the soft sand, and ran for the big silver train marked "CUBA" that had been waiting for us since we left. When we got inside the train we discovered that the women still hadn't gotten back, so we sat quietly in the luxurious leather seats slowly sipping rum. The women arrived an hour later.

While we were waiting in Yara, soldiers and units of militia began to arrive in the small town and squat all around the four or five sets of tracks waiting for their own trains. Most of them went back in boxcars, while we visitors had the luxury of the semi-air-conditioned coach.

The ride back was even longer than the fourteen

hours it took us before. Once when we stopped for water, we sat about two hours. Later, we stopped to pick up lunches. The atmosphere in the train was much the same as before, especially the Mexican delegates who whooped it up constantly. They even made a conga line up and down the whole length of the train. The young Mexican woman and I did a repeat performance also and talked most of the fifteen or sixteen hours it took us to get back to Habana. She was gentler with me this time, calling me "Yanqui imperialist" only a few times.

Everyone in the train was dirty, thirsty, and tired when it arrived in Habana. I had been wearing the same clothes for three days and hadn't even once taken off my shoes. The women were in misery. I hadn't seen a pocket mirror since the cattle cars.

The terminal looked like a rear outpost of some battlefield. So many people in filthy wrinkled clothes scrambling wearily out of trains. But even as tired as I was I felt excited at the prospect of being back in the big city for five more days. I was even more excited by the amount of thinking the trip to the Sierra was forcing me to. The "new" ideas that were being shoved at me, some of which I knew would be painful when I eventually got to New York.

The idea of "a revolution" had been foreign to me. It was one of those inconceivably "romantic" and/or hopeless ideas that we Norteamericanos have been taught since public school to hold up to the cold light of "reason." That reason being whatever repugnant lie our usurious "ruling class" had paid their journalists to disseminate. The reason that allows that voting, in a country where the parties are exactly the same, can be made to assume the gravity of actual moral engagement. The reason that permits a young intellectual to believe he has said something profound when he says, "I don't trust men in uniforms." The *residue* had settled on all our lives, and no one can function comfortably in this country without it. That thin crust of lie we cannot even detect in our own thinking. That rotting of the mind which had enabled us to think about Hiroshima as if someone else had done it, or to believe vaguely that the "counter-revolution" in Guatemala was an "internal" affair.

The rebels among us have become merely people like myself who grow beards and will not participate in politics. Drugs, juvenile deliquency, complete isolation from the vapid mores of the country, a few current ways out. But name an alternative here. Something not inextricably bound up in a lie. Something not part of liberal stupidity or the actual filth of vested interest. There is none. It's much too late. We are an *old* people already. Even the vitality of our art is like bright flowers growing up through a rotting carcass.

But the Cubans, and the other *new* peoples (in Asia, Africa, South America) don't need us, and we had better stay out of their way.

I came out of the terminal into the street and stopped at a newsstand to buy a paper. The headlines of one Miami paper read, "CUBAN CELEBRATION RAINED OUT." I walked away from the stand as fast as I could.

1961

letter to jules feiffer

August 28

Dear Mr. Feiffer,

Unfortunately, I don't have your letter to Mr. Richard Gibson, which appeared in the *Voice* a few weeks ago, in front of me, so I can't refer directly to it, but I remember when I read that letter it made me furious.

If I remember correctly, you made some terribly campy remarks about Mr. Gibson's use of the phrase "self-styled," as to the correctness (?) or motive(s) for its use. I also remember your making some disparaging remarks about Robert Williams and his struggle with the Klan, as well as his newsletter, *The Crusader*, which I think you termed a "hate sheet." I also think you questioned (?) the use of the term *Afro-American* and made another camp about it being "in" this year, etc. I definitely remember that you ended the letter "We Judeo-

Americans stand confused," or something like that.

As for the use of the term "self-styled," I would say that Mr. Gibson is wrong on that point. You, for one, and Mr. Harrington, whom I must assume you were defending, are most of all *not* self-styled—liberals or anything else for that matter. Were your liberalism, or the liberalism that Mr. Harrington so vacuously posits, of a truly self-styled nature it would not sound so depressingly familiar. It would, at least, have some of the originality that a few of your cartoons somehow manage to impart. The fact is that most of the *would-be* (is that a better phrase?) American liberals seem for the most part to fall out of a mold so fixed and predictable that they have become almost completely "neutralized" as far as the political life of this country is concerned. They have also developed into the most viciously wrong-headed group of amateur social theorists extant. They, or rather, you, liberals, are people with extremely heavy consciences and almost nonexistent courage. Too little is always enough. And it is always the symbol, the token, that appeals to you most. For the Feiffer/Harrington/*Village Voice* liberal, the single futile housing project in a jungle of slums and disease eases your conscience, so you are loudest in praising it. The single black student in the Southern University, the promoted porter in Marietta, Georgia—all ease the liberal's conscience like a benevolent but highly addictive drug. And for them, you, "moderation" is a kind of religious catch phrase that you are liable to be caught mumbling on street corners, even alone, late at night.

The new countries of Asia, Africa, and Latin America are not interested in your shallow conscience-saving slogans and protests of moderation or "political guarantees." As a character in Burroughs' *Naked Lunch* says, "You think I am innarested to contact your horrible old condition? I am not innarested at all." And however the governments of these countries evolve, whatever political structures they set up, you had better get used to the idea that they will not evolve into the parliamentary procedures of our local chamber of commerce. If you want "self-determination" for these countries, but are afraid of "the Communist menace," you'd better ask yourself if that "menace" exists anywhere in the world except the Western bloc? These new countries don't have to be afraid of Communism; probably it, or some other form of socialism, is the only economic proclivity that will insure them freedom. Freedom, that is, from exploitation at the hands of this "bastion of freedom." The problems of most of the peoples in the world have, unfortunately, only very slightly to do with "freedom of the press" or "political guarantees." Most people cannot read their own languages and have never voted. Their problems are usually things we do not even question, *i.e.*, enough to eat, clothes to wear, a decent place to live, a livelihood. And no amount of thin-willed middle-headed talk about *moderation* is going to ease any of these ills. Fidel Castro, Kwame N'Krumah, Sukarno, Nasser, and some others have actually done something about these ills, in their own countries. And they certainly don't have enough time to worry about what some well-off merchant's son, whose sole idea of moral engagement is *voting*, in a country where the political parties are exactly the same, has to say about the way they are conducting the resurrection of their people.

As far as your terming *The Crusader* a "hate sheet," perhaps your memory is failing. Afro-Americans (Negroes, spades, shades, boots, woogies, *etc.*) in this country can afford, I believe, the luxury of hate. They certainly have enough to hate. Robert Williams, the NAACP leader in Monroe, North Carolina, definitely has enough to hate. A much decorated ex-marine who served "his country" in Korea, he returns home and now finds himself being shot at because he assumed he could exercise a few more of the privileges of American citizenship, that is, other than being drafted. I think I remember your saying something about being "distressed" (was that the word?) at the suggestion that Negroes would follow Williams' example. Well, buddy, you can be distressed as much as you please. In fact, I am in favor of no kind of Negro protest that does not distress the kind of ethical sterility your and Mr. Harrington's liberalism represents. Were you distressed because here for the first time Negroes, led by Mr. Williams, fought back when they were assaulted by Klansmen? (I can think of 5,000,000 people who used to live in Europe, who should've fought back when they were assaulted by racists. Can't you?) There is a growing number of Negroes who are not willing to be bashed over the head or have their houses bombed to prove that Mr. Gandhi was right. Again, I get the feeling that somehow liberals think that they are peculiarly qualified to tell American Negroes and the other oppressed peoples of the world how to wage their struggles. No one wants to hear it. They've heard enough of those benevolent fate tales before. As Nat Cole once said, "Your story's mighty touching, but it sounds like a lie."

The term *Afro-American*, which I will use or not use, as I please, is in growing usage among Negroes, and again it escapes me why you think you should have something to say about the desirability of its use, etc. A great many black people feel that *Afro-American* is an historically and ethnically correct term and that it is preferable to the word *Negro*, which is, after all, an *adjective*. Also, there has never been any clamor raised over other peoples' ethnic hyphenations, e.g., Italian (or Italo-) Americans, Irish-Americans, etc. Why so much fuss about Negroes wanting to call themselves Afro-Americans? And if you want to call yourself a Judeo (Judaeo?) American, it's perfectly all right with me. In fact, I think that if perhaps there were more Judeo-Americans and a few less bland, cultureless, middle-headed AMERICANS, this country might still be a great one.

Sincerely,
LeRoi Jones

1962

tokenism: 300 years for five cents

In Marietta, Georgia, the Lockheed Airplane people maintain a plant that employs more than 10,000 people, only a few of whom are black people. As is customary in the South, all the black people who work in that Lockheed plant work at menial jobs such as porters, messengers, haulers, etc. Recently, however, the national office of the NAACP and the Federal Government have been chiding the Lockheed people to hire Negroes in capacities other than the traditional porter-messenger syndrome. And I suppose it is a credit to those organizations that they finally did get Lockheed to concur with their wishes; in fact, the Marietta plant promoted one of their Negro porters to a clerical position. This move was hailed by the Federal Government, the NAACP, and similar secret societies as "a huge step forward in race relations" (to quote from the *New York Times*). The Negro who received the promotion, thus becoming "a symbol of American determination to rid itself of the stigma of racial discrimination" (*op. cit.*), was shown smiling broadly (without his broom) and looking generally symbolic. The *Times* added that this promotion and this symbolic move toward "racial understanding" also gives the ex-porter a five-cents-an-hour increase, or two dollars more a week. This means that instead of forty-five dollars a week (if, indeed, the porter made that much) this blazing symbol of social progress now makes forty-seven dollars a week.

There are almost 20,000,000 Negroes in the United States. One of these 20 million has been given a two-dollar raise and promoted to a clerical job that my two-year-old daughter could probably work out without too much trouble. And we are told that this act is *symbolic* of the "gigantic strides the Negro has taken since slavery."

In 1954, the Supreme Court ruled that segregated schools were illegal, and that, indeed, segregation in public schools should be wiped out "with all deliberate speed." Since 1954, this ruling has affected about 6.9 per cent of the nearly 4,000,000 Negro students in Southern segregated schools, and there are four states, Mississippi, South Carolina, Georgia, and Alabama, who have ignored the ruling entirely. And yet, here again, we are asked to accept the ruling itself (with its hypocritical double-talk—what is "all deliberate speed"?) as yet another example of "the gigantic strides," etc. The fact that the ruling affects only 6.9 per cent of 4,000,000 Negro students in the South (and this percentage stands greatly boosted by the inclusion of figures from the "liberal" border states such as Maryland, Missouri, and the

District of Columbia—in fact Maryland and the District account for *more than half* of the total percentage) apparently does not matter to the liberals and other eager humanists who claim huge victories in their "ceaseless war on inequality."

Negroes have been in this country since the early part of the seventeenth century. And they have only "legally" been free human beings since the middle of the nineteenth. So we have two hundred years of complete slavery and now for the last one hundred years a "legal" freedom that has so many ands, ifs, or buts that I, for one, cannot accept it as freedom at all but see it as a legal fiction that has been perpetuated to assuage the occasional loud rumbles of moral conscience that must at times smite all American white men.

These last hundred years, according to our official social chiropractors, have been for American Negroes years of progress and advancement. As *Time* magazine said, "Never has the Negro been able to purchase so much and never has he owned so much, free and clear." That is, everything but his own soul. It is not "progress" that the majority of Negroes want, but Freedom. And I apologize if that word, Freedom, sounds a little too unsophisticated or a little too much like 1930's social renascence for some people; the fact remains that it is the one thing that has been most consistently denied the Negro in America (as well as black men all over the world).

Self-determination is the term used when referring to some would-be nation's desire for freedom. The right to choose one's own path. The right to become exactly what one thinks himself capable of. And it strikes me as monstrous that a nation or, for that matter, a civilization like our Western civilization, reared for the last five hundred years exclusively in the humanistic bombast of the Renaissance, should find it almost impossible to understand the strivings of enslaved peoples to free themselves. It is this kind of paradox that has caused the word "Nationalism" to be despised and/or feared in the West, or shrugged off in official circles as "just another Communist plot." Even here in the United States the relatively mild attempts at "integration" in the South are met by accusations of being Communist-inspired. (And I would add as, say, a note of warning to the various Southern congressmen whose sole qualification for office is that they are more vociferous in their disparagement of Negroes than their opponents, that if they persist in crediting the Communists with every attempt at delivering the black American out of his real and constant bondage, someone's going to believe them . . . namely the new or aspirant nations of Asia, Latin America, and Africa.)

2

Actual slavery in the United States was supposed to have been brought to an end by the Civil War. There is rather bitter insistence in the point that it was *Americans* who were supposedly being freed; the African slaves had long since become American slaves. But it is by now almost a truism to point out that there was much more at stake in that war than the emancipation of the slaves. The Civil War, or at least the result of the Civil War, was undoubtedly the triumph of the Northern industrial classes over the Southern agricultural classes. As so many writers have termed it, "the triumph of American capitalism." The small oligarchy of American industrial capital had overcome its last great enemy, the rich Southern planter, and was now more or less free to bring the very processes of American government under its control.

But on the surface the Civil War looked like a great moral struggle out of which the side of right and justice had emerged victorious. The emancipation of Negroes, the passage, by the Republican Congress, of the 13th, 14th and 15th amendments (to give a "legal basis" for black citizenship), and the setting up of the Reconstruction governments in the South, all gave promise that a new era had arrived for Negroes. And in fact it had, but was of a complexion which was not immediately apparent, and was certainly not the new era most Negroes would have looked forward to.

The Reconstruction governments fell because the Northern industrialists joined with the planter classes of the South to disfranchise the Negro once again, frightened that a "coalition" of the poor and disfranchised Southern whites—the agrarian interests—and the newly freed Negroes might prove too strong a threat to their designs of absolute political and economic control of the South. As E. Franklin Frazier points out in *Black Bourgeosie*, "When agrarian unrest among the 'poor whites' of the South joined forces with the Populist movement, which represented the general unrest among American farmers, the question of race was used to defeat the co-operation of 'poor whites' and Negroes. It was then that the demagogues assumed leadership of the 'poor whites' and provided a solution of the class conflict among whites that offered no challenge to the political power and economic privileges of the industrialists and the planter class. The program, which made the Negro the scapegoat, contained the following provisions: (1) The Negro was completely disfranchised by all sorts of legal subterfuges, with the threat of force in the background; (2) the funds which were appropriated on a per capita basis for Negro school children were diverted to white schools; and (3) a legal system of segregation in all phases of public life was instituted. In order to justify this program, the demagogues, who were supported by the white propertied classes, engaged for twenty-five years in a campaign to prove that the Negro was subhuman, morally de-generate and intellectually incapable of being educated."

3

Tokenism, or what I define as the setting up of social stalemates or the extension of meager privilege to some few "selected" Negroes in order that a semblance of compromise or "progress," or a lessening in racial repression, might seem to be achieved, while actually helping to maintain the status quo just as rigidly, could not, of course, really come into being until after the emancipation. Before that, there was no real need to extend even a few tokens to the slave. There was, indeed, no reason why anyone had to create the illusion for the slave that he was "making progress," or governing himself, or any other such untruth. In a sense, however, the extension of "special privileges" to Negro house servants ("house niggers") did early help to create a new *class* of Negro, within the slave system. The "house nigger" not only assimilated "massa's" ideas and attitudes at a rapid rate, but his children were sometimes allowed to learn trades and become artisans and craftsmen. And it was these artisans and craftsmen who made up the bulk of the 500,000 black "freedmen" extant at the beginning of the Civil War.

The Reconstruction governments are the first actual example of the kind of crumb-dropping that was to characterize the Federal Government's attitude regarding the status of the "free" Negro. The Reconstruction governments were nothing but symbols, since no real lands were ever given to the Negroes, and even any political influence which had come to the ex-slaves as part of the Reconstruction was nullified by 1876 (the so-called redemption of the South).

Another aspect of tokenism is the setting apart or appointing of "leaders" among Negroes who in effect glorify whatever petty symbol the white ruling classes think is necessary for Negroes to have at that particular time. So, at the fall of the Reconstruction governments, the industrialist-financier-planter oligarchy found an able "leader" in Booker T. Washington, a Negro through whom these interests could make their wishes known to the great masses of Negroes. After the North had more or less washed its hands of the whole "Southern mess," and it was a generally accepted idea that the Negroes had ruined the Reconstruction simply because they were incapable of governing themselves, Booker T. Washington came into great prominence and influence as a Negro leader because he accepted the idea of segregation as a "solution" to the race problem, and also because he advocated that Negroes learn trades rather than go into any of the more ambitious professions.

"Coming from Booker T. Washington, who enjoyed entré into the society of Standard Oil executives, railroad magnates, and Andrew Carnegie, the strategy was persuasive. Washington avowed his loyalty to laissez faire, took his stand in the South as a southerner, and accepted social inequality for the forseeable future. Blocked by the power of the whites and told by their own spokesman that 'white leadership is preferable,' most Negroes followed . . ." (from *The Contours Of American History*, W. A. Williams, 1961).

The wealth and influence of the great industrialists backed the Washington solution and as Williams points out, "Washington's position was made almost impregnable through the generosity of northern white philanthropists who liked his ideology (which included a code of labor quietism and even strikebreaking)." Negro intellectuals like W. E. B. DuBois who attacked Washington's position had little chance to shake it, opposed by such formidable opponents as the monied interests and the philanthropists, who replaced the "radical republican" idea of actually redistributing land to the freed Negroes with ineffective philanthropies such as Howard University or Tuskeegee (which was Booker T.'s pet—a college for Negroes that taught trades, *e.g.*, carpentry, masonry). And of course, as it was intended, the tokens did very little to improve the general conditions of Negroes anywhere. The Sumner-Stevens plan of redistributing land among the freedmen, in fact even breaking up the large plantations and making small farms for both white and black, would have changed the entire history of this country had it been implemented in good faith. But such an idea definitely proved a threat to the hold of the planters and industrialists over the politics and economy of the South. So it was defeated.

4

Radicals like DuBois (who left Atlanta University so he would not embarrass them with his opinions) helped set up the National Association for the Advancement of Colored People in 1909. At that time the organization was considered extremely radical, and it was merely asking—but for the first time—for "complete equality." Most of the financiers and philanthropists who made a sometime hobby out of extending stale crumbs to Negroes denounced the organization. Also, most of the so-called Negro middle class could not abide by the radicalism of the organization's program, and some of them (the Negro educators in particular, who depended on the philanthropists for their bread, butter, and prestige) brought as much pressure as they could on the fledgling NAACP to modify its policies. (And I think it is not too violent a digression to ask just what kind of men or what kind of desperation would have to be inflicted upon a man's soul in order for him to say that giving him equal rights in his own country is "too radical"? E. Franklin Frazier does a very good job in *Black Bourgeosie* of describing the type of man who would be capable of such social pathology.) But radicalism or no, when the First World War ended and the great exodus of Negroes from the South began, membership in the NAACP grew tremendously. Yet despite the great support the NAACP received from the Negro masses in its incunabula, the organization was more and more influenced by its white liberal supporters and gradually modified its program and position to that of the white middle class, thereby swiftly limiting its appeal to the middle-class Negro. Today, the NAACP is almost completely out of touch with the great masses of blacks and bases its programs on a "liberal" middle-class line, which affects only a very tiny portion of the 20,000,000 Negroes living in the United States. It has, in fact, become little more than a token itself.

5

A rich man told me recently that a liberal is a man who tells other people what to do with their money. I told him that that was right from the side of the telescope he looked through, but that as far as I was concerned a liberal was a man who told other people what to do with their poverty.

I mention this peculiarly American phenomenon, i.e., American Liberalism, because it is just this group of amateur social theorists, American Liberals, who have done most throughout American history to insure the success of tokenism. Whoever has proposed whatever particular social evasion or dilution—to whatever ignominious end—it is usually the liberal who gives that lie the greatest lip service. They, liberals, are people with extremely heavy consciences and almost nonexistent courage. Too little is always enough. And it is always the *symbol* that appeals to them most. The single futile housing project in the jungle of slums and disease eases the liberals' conscience, so they are loudest in praising it—even though it might not solve any problems at all. The single black student in the Southern university, the promoted porter in Marietta, Georgia—all ease the liberals' conscience like a benevolent but highly addictive drug. And, for them, "moderation" is a kind of religious catch phrase that they are wont to mumble on street corners even alone late at night.

Is it an excess for a man to ask to be free? To declare, even vehemently, that no man has the right to dictate the life of another man? Is it so radical and untoward for nations to claim the right of self-determination? Freedom *now!* has become the cry of a great many American Negroes and colonial nations. Not freedom "when you get ready to give it," as some spurious privilege or shabby act of charity; but *now!* The liberal says, "You are a radical." So be it.

Liberals, as good post-Renaissance men, believe wholeheartedly in *progress.* There are even those people who speak knowingly about "progress in the arts." But progress is not, and never has been, the question as far as the enslaving of men is concerned. Africans never asked to be escorted to the New World. They never had any idea that learning "good English" and wearing shoes had anything to do with the validity of their lives on earth. Slavery was not anything but an unnecessarily cruel and repressive method of making money for the Western white man. Colonialism was a more subtle, but equally repressive method of accomplishing the same end. The liberal is in a strange position because his conscience, unlike the conscience of his richer or less intelligent brothers, has always bothered him about these acts, but never sufficiently to move him to any concrete action except the setting up of palliatives and symbols to remind him of his own good faith. In fact, even though the slave trade, for instance, was entered into for purely commercial reasons, after a few years the more liberal-minded Americans began to try to justify it as a method of converting heathens to Christianity. (And, again, you can see how perfect Christianity was for the slave then; a great number of slave uprisings were dictated by the Africans' gods or the new slaves' desire to return to the land of their gods. As I put it in a recent essay on the sociological development of blues: "You can see how necessary, how perfect, it was that Christianity came first, that the African was given something 'to take his mind off Africa,' that he was forced, if he still wished to escape the filthy paternalism and cruelty of slavery, to wait at least until he died, when he could be transported peacefully and majestically to 'the promised land.'" I'm certain the first Negro spirituals must have soothed a lot of consciences as well as enabling a little more relaxation among the overseers. It almost tempts me toward another essay tentatively titled *Christianity as a Deterrent to Slave Uprisings*. More tokens.

A Negro who is told that the "desegregation" of a bus terminal in Georgia somehow represents "progress" is definitely being lied to. Progress to where? The bare minimum of intelligent life is what any man wants. This was true in 1600 when the first slaves were hauled off the boats, and it has not changed. Perhaps the trappings and the external manifestations that time and the lessons of history have proposed make some things seem different or changed in the world, but the basic necessities of useful life are the same. If a tractor has replaced a mule, the need to have the field produce has not changed. And if a black man can speak English now, or read a newspaper, whereas (ask any liberal) he could not in

18 so-and-so, he is no better off now than he was then if he still cannot receive the basic privileges of manhood. In fact, he is perhaps worse off than in 18 so-and-so since he is now being constantly persuaded that he *is* receiving these basic privileges (or, at least, he is told that he soon will, *e.g.*, R. Kennedy's high comic avowal that perhaps in forty years a Negro might be president).

But, for me, the idea of "progress" is a huge fallacy. An absurd Western egoism that has been foisted on the rest of the world as an excuse for slavery and colonialism. An excuse for making money. Because this progress the Western slavemaster is always talking about means simply the mass acquisition of all the dubious fruits of the industrial revolution. And the acquisition of material wealth has, in my mind, only very slightly to do with self-determination or freedom. Somehow, and most especially in the United States, the fact that more Negroes can buy new Fords this year than they could in 1931 is supposed to represent some great stride *forward*. To where? How many new Fords will Negroes have to own before police in Mississippi stop using police dogs on them? How many television sets and refrigerators will these same Negroes have to own before they are allowed to vote without being made to live in tents, or their children allowed decent educations? And even if a bus station in Anniston, Alabama, is "integrated," how much does this help reduce the 25 per cent unemployment figure that besets Negroes in Harlem?

If, right this minute, I were, in some strange fit of irrationality, to declare that "I am a free man and have the right of complete self-determination," chances are that I would be dead or in jail by nightfall. But being an American Negro, I am supposed to be conditioned to certain "unfortunate" aspects of American democracy. And all my reactions are supposedly based on this conditioning, which is, in effect, that even as a native born American, etc., etc., there are certain things I cannot do because I have a black skin. Tokenism is that philosophy (of psychological exploitation) which is supposed to assuage my natural inclinations toward complete freedom. For the middle-class Negro this assuagement can take the form it takes in the mainstream of American life, *i.e.*, material acquisition, or the elevating of one "select" coon to some position that seems heaped in "prestige," *e.g.*, Special Delegate to the United Nations, Director of Public Housing, Assistant Press Secretary to the President of the United States, Vice President in Charge of Personnel for Chock Full 'O Nuts, Borough President of Manhattan, etc. The "Speaking of People" column in *Ebony* magazine is the banal chronicler of such "advances," *e.g.*, the first Negro sheriff of Banwood, Utah, or the first Negro Asst. Film Editor for BRRR films. But the lower-class Negro cannot use this kind of tokenism, so he is pretty much left in the lurch. But so effective is this kind of crumb-dropping among the *soi-disant* black middle class that these people become the actual tokens themselves, or worse. Thus when an issue like the treacherous relief cuts in Newburgh, New York, presents itself, the black middle class is actually likely to side with reactionaries, even though, as in the Newburgh case, such a situation harms a great many poorer Negroes. This kind of process reaches perhaps its most absurd, albeit horrible, manifestation when a man like George Schuyler, in the Negro paper *The Pittsburgh Courier*, can write editorials *defending the Portuguese* in Angola, even after the United States Government itself had been pressured into censuring this NATO ally. It is also a man like Schuyler who is willing to support one of the great aphorisms of tokenism (this one begun by the worst elements of racist neo-colonialism) that somehow a man, usually a black man, must "make progress to freedom." That somehow, a man must show he is "*ready* for independence or self-determination." A man is either free or he is not. There cannot be any apprenticeship for freedom. My God, what makes a black man, in America or Africa, or any of the other oppressed colonial peoples of the world, less ready for freedom than the average *Daily News* reading American white man?

But again, while it is true that there is a gulf of tokens seemingly separating the middle-class Negro from the great masses of Negroes (just as there is seemingly a great gulf of tokens separating the "select cadre" of a great many colonial countries from their oppressed people), I insist that it is only an artificial separation, and that the black bourgeosie (and their foreign cousins) are no better off than the poorest Negro in this country. But how to tell the *first* Negro Asst. Film Editor of BRRR films that he is just as bad off as the poorest and most oppressed of his black brothers? Tokenism is no abstract philosophy; it was put into action by hard-headed realists.

But realists or no, there is in the world now among most of its oppressed peoples a growing disaffection with meaningless platitudes, and a reluctance to be had by the same shallow phrases that have characterized the hypocritical attitude of the West toward the plight of the American black man and all colonial peoples. There will be fewer and fewer tragedies like the murder of Patrice Lumumba. The new nations will no longer allow themselves to be sucked in by these same hackneyed sirens of tokenism or malevolent liberalism. The world, my friends, is definitely changing.

"black" is a country

To a growing list of "dirty" words that make Americans squirm add the word *Nationalism*. I would say that the word has gained almost as much infamy in some quarters of this country as that all-time anathema and ugliness, *Communism*. In fact, some journalists, commentators, and similar types have begun to use the two words interchangeably. It goes without saying that said commentators, etc., and the great masses of Americans who shudder visibly at the mention of those words cannot know what they mean. And it is certainly not my function, here, to rectify that situation completely. But I do think that unless the great majority of people in this country begin to understand just exactly what Nationalism is (or at least that variety of Nationalism which is most in evidence among the smaller, so-called uncommitted countries of the world) they will pass from the scene like the boxer who "never knew what hit him."

The concept of "acting in one's own best interests" is certainly not unknown to America or to the rest of the so-called Free World (which I am told includes Portugal, South Africa, and parts of Mississippi). In fact, I would say it is just this concept which has allowed the Western peoples to remain for so long the richest and best-fed in the world. No matter what people or countries had ultimately to suffer while they were pursuing these "best interests," the pragmatic efficiency of England, France, or the United States in accomplishing such ends is almost legendary. Weird historical "music," in the so-called Opium Wars in China (Britain), the "defense" of the Suez Canal (Britain/France), the Spanish-American and Castro-American Wars (United States)—some examples, both recent and long past, of this "best interests" doctrine as applied by the West— leaps immediately to mind. And these kinds of activities can also be included within the definition of *Nationalism*. So it seems strange at first to see Westerners squirming at the mention of a concept and/or practice they themselves have been most responsible for perfecting. There is a comic analogy in the fact that in con man language "savage" means "sucker."

The "rub," of course, is that when another people or country, who have been used or exploited because it served the best interests of a Western power, suddenly become politically and/or physically powerful enough to begin talking about *their* own best interests, which of course are usually in direct opposition to the wishes of their exploiters, it is then that *Nationalism* becomes a dirty word—one to be stricken from as many minds as possible, by whatever methods. (To my mind, it is absurd to think for a moment that the people who killed Patrice Lumumba thought he was a Communist. They understood exactly what he was.) And it seems a simple enough conclusion to me that most of the so-called "hotspots" in the world are caused by this same conflict of "nationalisms," even in our own South. (An historical aside: The Civil War in the United States was of course the victory of the industrial interests in the country over the agricultural—a kind of nationalism. For these same reasons, any white racist in the South today who suddenly, for whatever hypothetical reasons, became strong enough to convince some large part of the white South that secession was the only way to solve the South's problems would be disposed of by the tobacco people, etc., in short order. More "Nationalism." The conflict of interests.)

What I am driving at is the fact that to me the Africans, Asians, and Latin Americans who are news today because of their nationalism, i.e., the militant espousal of the doctrine of serving one's own people's interests before those of a foreign country, e.g., the United States, are exactly the examples the black man in this country should use in his struggle for *independence*. (And that is what the struggle remains, for independence—from the political, economic, social, spiritual, and psychological domination of the white man. Put more simply, the struggle moves to make certain that no man has the right to dictate the life of another man. The struggle is not simply for "equality," or "better jobs," or "better schools," and the rest of those half-hearted liberal clichés; it is to completely *free* the black man from the domination of the white man. Nothing else. The man who asks the question "Would You Let Your Daughter Marry One?" must realize that that question is generally outmoded. The question now for those same people becomes "What Would I Do If One Turned My Daughter Down?" It is the freedom to make the choice that is my insistence, and the insistence, I hope, of most black Americans.) And it is the new nationalists everywhere who are pointing out dramatically the road our own struggle must take. In America, black *is* a country. The Cubans are attacked by this country because they refuse to let themselves be used solely to further the Industrial interests of this country. Communism is *not* the issue. Lumumba was killed because he resisted the designs of the neo-colonialists to continue to make *money* from the labors of the African. Communism, again, was not the issue.

The black man has been separated and made to live in his own country of color. If you are black the only roads into the mainland of American life are through subservience, cowardice, and loss of manhood. Those are the white man's roads. It is time we built our own. America is as much a black country as a white one. The lives and destinies of the white American are bound up inextricably with those of the black American, even though the latter has been forced for hundreds of years to inhabit the lonely country of black. It is time we impressed the white man with the nature of his ills, as well as the nature of our own. The Negro's struggle in America is only a microcosm of the struggle of the new countries all over the world.

The idea of "passive" resistance is not the answer. It is an Indian "rope trick" that cannot be applied in this scientific country. No one believes in magic anymore. The Christian church cannot help us. The new nationalists all over the world have learned to be suspicious of "Christianity." Christ and the Dollar Sign have gotten mixed up in their minds, and they *know* that the latter is their enemy. It is time black Americans got those two confused as well. The idea of the "all black society" within the superstructure of an all white society is useless as well (even if it were possible). We *are* Americans, which is our strength as well as our desperation. The struggle is for *independence*, not separation—or assimilation for that matter. Do what you want to with *your* life . . . when you can. I want to be independent of black men just as much as I want independence from the white. It is just that achieving the latter involves all black men, or at least those who have not already taken those available roads into the mainstream I mentioned earlier—subservience, cowardice, and loss of manhood.

This struggle has first got to aim itself at those black men who have already taken those three roads to "success." The "rubber stamps" of our exploitation. Usually, as we know, these rubber stamps are set up as our "leaders." Official Negroes they are called. Good. Let them be official. It only means that they are as sick and useless as everything else in this country that has, of recent years, been unofficial. When we speak of the ugliness of American foreign policy, we cannot separate our disgust with that from the knowledge that these official Negroes, as such, must be the repositories of those same policies. The best interests of the black man in America cannot be furthered by these puppets and messengers. It is not in the best interests of the black man if another black man gets up in the United Nations and apologizes to that august body for the conduct of "his people." It is not in the best interests of the black American if another black American suggests to the world that the only way in which his people are going to achieve their independence is to get walked on in public places or blown out of buses. And it is strictly up to those black people who realize these things to come out and say them. Not only say them, but act upon them. And we must act now, in what I see as an extreme "nationalism," *i.e.*, in the best interests of our country, the name of which the rest of America has pounded into our heads for four hundred years, *Black*.

city of harlem

In a very real sense, Harlem is the capital of Black America. And America has always been divided into black and white, and the substance of the division is social, economic, and cultural. But even the name Harlem, now, means simply Negroes (even though some other peoples live there too). The identification is international as well: even in Belize, the capital of predominantly Negro British Honduras, there are vendors who decorate their carts with flowers and the names or pictures of Negro culture heroes associated with Harlem like Sugar Ray Robinson. Some of the vendors even wear T-shirts that say "Harlem, U.S.A.," and they speak about it as a black Paris. In Havana a young Afro-Cuban begged me to tell him about the "big leg ladies" of Lenox Avenue, hoping, too, that I could provide some way for him to get to that mystic and romantic place.

There are, I suppose, contained within the central mythology of Harlem, almost as many versions of its glamour, and its despair, as there are places with people to make them up. (In one meaning of the name, Harlem is simply a place white cab drivers will not go.) And Harlem means not only Negroes, but, of course, whatever other associations one might connect with them. So in one breath Harlem will be the pleasure-happy center of the universe, full of loud, hippy mamas in electric colors and their fast, slick-head papas, all of them twisting and grinning in the streets in a kind of existential joyousness that never permits of sadness or responsibility. But in another breath this same place will be the gathering place for every crippling human vice, and the black men there simply victims of their own peculiar kind of sloth and childishness. But perhaps these are not such different versions after all; chances are both these stereotypes come from the same kinds of minds.

But Harlem, as it is, as it exists for its people, as an actual place where actual humans live—that is a very different thing. Though, to be sure, Harlem is a place—a city really—where almost anything any person could think of to say goes on, probably does go on, or has gone on, but like any other city, it must escape *any* blank generalization simply because it is alive, and changing each second with each breath any of its citizens take.

When Africans first got to New York, or New Amsterdam as the Dutch called it, they lived in the farthest downtown portions of the city, near what is now called The Bowery. Later, they shifted, and were shifted, as their numbers grew, to the section known as Greenwich Village. The Civil War Draft Riots in 1863 accounted for the next move by New York's growing Negro population.

After this violence (a few million dollars' worth of property was destroyed, and a Negro orphanage was burned to the ground) a great many Negroes moved across the river into Brooklyn. But many others moved farther uptown to an area just above what was known as Hell's Kitchen. The new Negro ghetto was known as Black Bohemia, and later, after the success of an all black regiment in the Spanish-American War, this section was called San Juan Hill. And even in the twenties when most Negroes had made their move even further uptown to Harlem, San Juan Hill was still a teeming branch office of black night life.

Three sections along the east side of Manhattan, The Tenderloin, Black Bohemia, and San Juan Hill or The Jungle featured all kinds of "sporting houses," cabarets, "dancing classes," afterhours gin mills, as well as the Gumbo Suppers, Fish Fries, Egg Nog Parties, Chitterlin' Struts, and Pigfoot Hops, before the Negroes moved still farther uptown.

The actual move into what is now Harlem was caused by quite a few factors, but there are a few that were particularly important as catalysts. First, locally, there were more race riots around the turn of the century between the white poor (as always) and the Negroes. Also, the Black Bohemia section was by now extremely overcrowded, swelled as it was by the influx of Negroes from all over the city. The section was a notorious red light district (but then there have only been two occupations a black woman could go into in America without too much trouble: the other was domestic help) and the overcrowding made worse by the moral squalor that poverty encourages meant that the growing local black population had to go somewhere. The immigrant groups living on both sides of the black ghetto fought in the streets to keep their own ghettoes autonomous and pure, and the Negro had to go elsewhere.

At this time, just about the turn of the century, Harlem (an area which the first Africans had helped connect with the rest of the Dutch city by clearing a narrow road—Broadway—up into the woods of Nieuw Haarlem)

was still a kind of semi-suburban area, populated, for the
most part, by many of the city's wealthiest families. The
elaborate estates of the eighteenth century, built by men
like Alexander Hamilton and Roger Morris, were still
being lived in, but by the descendants of wealthy mer-
chants. (The Hamilton house still stands near Morning-
side Heights, as an historic landmark called The Grange.
The Morris house, which was once lived in by Aaron
Burr, is known as The Jumel House, and it still stands at
the northern part of Harlem, near the Polo Grounds, as
a museum run by the D.A.R. George Washington used it
as his headquarters for a while during the Revolutionary
War.) So there was still the quiet elegance of the nineteenth century brownstones and spacious apartment
buildings, the wide drives, rolling greens, and huge-
trunked trees.

What made the area open up to Negroes was the
progress that America has always been proud of—an
elevated railway went up in the nineties, and the very
rich left immediately and the near rich very soon after.
Saint Philips Church, after having its old site bought up
by a railroad company, bought a large piece of property,
with large apartment buildings, in the center of Harlem,
and, baby, the panic was on. Rich and famous Negroes
moved into the vacated luxury houses very soon after,
including the area now known as "Strivers Row," which
was made up of almost one hundred brick mansions
designed by Stanford White. The panic was definitely
on—but still only locally.

What really turned that quiet suburb into "Black
Paris" was the coming of the First World War and the
mass exodus of Negroes from the South to large urban

centers. At the turn of the century most Negroes still lived in the South and were agricultural laborers, but the entrance of America into the War, and the desperate call for cheap unskilled labor, served to start thousands of Negroes scrambling North. The flow of immigrants from Europe had all but ceased by 1914, and the industrialists knew immediately where to turn. They even sent recruiters down into the South to entice the Negroes north. In 1900 the Negro population of New York City was 60,000; by 1920 it was 152,467; by 1930 it was 327,706. And most of these moved, of course, uptown.

It was this mass exodus during the early part of the century that was responsible for most of the black cities of the North—the huge Negro sections of New York, Chicago, Philadelphia, Detroit, etc. It was also responsible for what these sections would very shortly become, as the masses of Southern Negroes piled into their new Jordans, thinking to have a go at an innocent America.

The twenties are legend because they mark America's sudden insane entrance into the 20th century. The war had brought about a certain internationalism and prosperity (even, relatively speaking, for Negroes). During the twenties Harlem was the mecca of the good time and in many ways even came to symbolize the era called the Jazz Age. Delirious white people made the trip uptown to hear Negro musicians and singers, and watch Negro dancers, and even Negro intellectuals. It was, I suppose, the black man's debut into the most sophisticated part of America. The old darkies of the plantation were suddenly all over the North, and making a whole lot of noise.

There were nightclubs in Harlem that catered only to

white audiences, but with the best Negro entertainers. White intellectuals made frequent trips to Harlem, not only to find out about a newly emerging black America, but to party with an international set of swinging bodies. It was the era of Ellington at The Cotton Club for the sensual, and The New Negro for the intellectual. Everyone spoke optimistically of the Negro Renaissance, and The New Negro, as if, somehow, the old Negro wasn't good enough. Harlem sparkled then, at least externally, and it took the depression to dull that sparkle, and the long lines of unemployed Negroes and the longer lines at the soup kitchens and bread queues brought reality down hard on old and new Negroes alike. So the tourist trade diminished, and colorful Harlem became just a social liability for the white man, and an open air jail for the black.

The cold depression thirties, coupled with the decay of old buildings and ancient neighborhoods, and, of course, the seeming inability of the "free enterprise" system to provide either jobs or hope for a great many black people in the city of Harlem, have served to make this city another kind of symbol. For many Negroes, whether they live in Harlem or not, the city is simply a symbol of naked oppression. You can walk along 125th Street any evening and meet about one hundred uniformed policemen, who are there, someone will tell you, to protect the people from themselves.

For many Negroes Harlem is a place one escapes from, and lives in shame about for the rest of his life. But this is one of the weirdest things about the American experience, that it can oppress a man, almost suck his life away, and then make him so ashamed that he was among the oppressed, rather than the oppressors, that he will never offer any protest.

The legitimate cultural tradition of the Negro in Harlem (and America) is one of wild happiness, usually at some black man's own invention—of speech, of dress, of gait, the sudden twist of a musical phrase, the warmness or hurt of someone's voice. But that culture is also one of hatred and despair. Harlem must contain all of this and be capable of producing all of these emotions.

People line the streets in summer—on the corners or hanging out the windows—or head for other streets in winter. Vendors go by slowly . . . and crowds of people from movies or church. (Saturday afternoons, warm or cold, 125th is jammed with shoppers and walkers, and the record stores scream through loudspeakers at the street.) Young girls, doctors, pimps, detectives, preachers, drummers, accountants, gamblers, labor organizers, postmen, wives, Muslims, junkies, the employed, and the unemployed: all going someplace—an endless stream of Americans, whose singularity in America is that they are black and can never honestly enter into the lunatic asylum of white America.

Harlem for this reason is a community of nonconformists, since any black American, simply by virtue of his blackness, is weird, a nonconformist in this society. A community of nonconformists, not an artists' colony—though blind "ministers" still wander sometimes along 137th Street, whispering along the strings of their guitars—but a colony of old-line Americans, who can hold out, even if it is a great deal of the time in misery and ignorance, but still hold out, against the hypocrisy and sterility of big-time America, and still try to make their own lives, simply because of their color, but by now, not so simply, because that color now does serve to identify people in America whose feelings about it are not broadcast every day on television.

cold, hurt, and sorrow
(streets of despair)

These streets stretch from one end of America to the other and connect like a maze from which very few can fully escape. Despair sits on this country in most places like a charm, but there is a special gray death that loiters in the streets of an urban Negro slum. And the men who walk those streets, tracing and retracing their steps to some hopeless job or a pitiful rooming house or apartment or furnished room, sometimes stagger under the weight of that gray, humiliated because it is not even "real."

Sometimes walking along among the ruined shacks and lives of the worst Harlem slum, there is a feeling that just around the next corner you'll find yourself in South Chicago or South Philadelphia, maybe even Newark's Third Ward. In these places life, and its possibility, has been distorted almost identically. And the distortion is as old as its sources: the fear, frustration, and hatred that Negroes have always been heir to in America. It is just that in the cities, which were once the black man's twentieth century "Jordan," *promise* is a dying bitch with rotting eyes. And the stink of her dying is a deadly killing fume.

The blues singers know all this. They knew before they got to the cities. "I'd rather drink muddy water, sleep in a hollow log, than be in New York City treated like a dirty dog." And when they arrived, in those various cities, it was much worse than even they had imagined. The city blues singers are still running all that down. Specifically, it's what a man once named for me unnatural adversity. It is social, it is economic, it is cultural and historical. Some of its products are emotional and psychological; some are even artistic, as if Negroes suffered better than anyone else. It's hard enough to be a human being under any circumstances, but when there is an entire civilization determined to stop you from being one, things get a little more desperately complicated. What do you do then?

You can stand in doorways late nights and hit people in the head. You can go to church Saturday nights and Sundays and three or four times during the week. You can stick a needle in your arm four or five times a day, and bolster the economy. You can buy charms and herbs and roots, or wear your hat backwards to keep things from getting worse. You can drink till screaming is not loud enough, and the coldest night is all right to sleep outside in. You can buy a big car . . . if the deal goes down. There's so much, then, you can do, to yourself, or to somebody else. Another man sings, "I'm drinkin' t.n.t., I'm smokin' dynamite, I hope some screwball starts a fight."

One can never talk about Harlem in purely social terms, though there are ghetto facts that make any honest man shudder. It is the tone, the quality of suffering each man knows as his own that finally must be important, but this is the most difficult thing to get to. (There are about twenty young people from one small Southern town, all friends, all living within the same few blocks of the black city, all of whom are junkies, communally hooked. What kind of statistic is *that*? And what can you say when you read it?)

The old folks kept singing, there will be a better day . . . or, the sun's gonna shine in my back door some day . . . or, I've had my fun if I don't get well no more. What did they want? What would that sun turn out to be?

Hope is a delicate suffering. Its waste products vary, but most of them are meaningful. And as a cat named Mean William once said, can you be glad, if you've never been sad?

street protest

There have been black men trying to get other black men to protest and rise against the weight of America's oppression since those first clipper ships bringing them in in chains. There have been black men willing even to die, and not for an abstract freedom they teach you in grammar school which belongs largely to dead patriots masquerading as Indians, but for the simple need to say exactly what they think, and explain exactly what they think America is. But any black American who ever tried to say something factual about the black man's life in America, even in the uncomplicated circumstance of slavery, was either killed or, as the slave ship grew more sophisticated and gave a few Negroes radios or air-conditioning in the hold, driven crazy or driven away for daring to protest.

But to a large extent America convinced itself that the black man didn't mind being a slave. (You remember those grinning woogies strumming on the cotton bales? The happy-go-lucky image of Harlem is an extension of this.) Although the records of slave revolts are too numerous to support such a faked conclusion, and men like Caesar, Gabriel, Denmark Vesey, Nat Turner, and so many others were not killed for strumming banjos.

Before the Negro came north at the beginning of the century there was not much room for any protest except one that would have to begin at violence. But the North offered at least a little more room to swing, buoyed up as it was, and is, by a kindly Liberal/Missionary syndrome that will let you say almost anything you want, as long as you don't threaten to *do* anything. (The missionary types would tell the more repressive Americans, "Such protest is good for business.")

But ever since the early years of this century there have been a great many formal Negro protest groups thriving in the North: not only the large, more respectable groups like the NAACP, but the quickly organized and usually quickly disbanded protest groups, who have no clearly outlined "program" and of course no wealthy supporters and therefore very little influence—except that they represent all the people with no influence.

Some men take it upon themselves, even alone, to make some noise about the filth they see. In Harlem such men are easy to hear; their persistence makes them available. They don't even need a soapbox and an American flag, or a place on the stand in front of Michaux's House Of Proper Propaganda on Seventh Avenue just above 125th Street. They just stand out somewhere and talk loud, and a few people stand and listen.

At an NAACP-Church rally recently, in front of the Hotel Theresa, where the large, money-financed, more organized "protests" take place, a single speaker took up a stand directly across the street from the main rally and tried to shout the electronic equipment down with a rolled-up magazine. There were about one hundred cops watching the main rally and about two watching the loner.

There are some protest speakers who wear African

robes and sandals, and study African history. And now, as Africa rises, there are some who speak of "teaching the children about their heritage," though they ought to know also that that heritage is one that is cruelly local.

Since the twenties there have been all kinds of local betterment leaders and social prophets in Harlem. Marcus Garvey was both, and even before he began his Back To Africa movement and the Universal Negro Improvement Association, he was shouting at people on Lenox Avenue to get themselves together and get the white man off their backs. The sentiment is still strong in Harlem, and leaflets and speakers urging Negroes to "Buy Black" are still ubiquitous. And now, young clean-headed, clean-suited boys wave their copies of *Muhammad Speaks*, spreading the word of Elijah Muhammad and Malcolm X.

Any weekend will find some speakers out, singly or encouraged—especially if the weather's good. There is always a picket line getting ready to form or a neophyte protest group, and there are always reasons why they should form. There are even some speakers with personal uniforms to specify their utopias. But an open and very public understanding of what all these protests are about has come to Harlem, just as it has come to Negroes throughout the rest of the country, whose local Harlems are equally impossible, equally repressive. In many cases, the men on the platforms are just repeating what they hear. From people's mouths, and people's horns.

soul food

Recently, a young Negro novelist writing in *Esquire* about the beauties of America mentioned that one of the things wrong with Negroes was that, unlike the Chinese, boots have neither a language of their own nor a characteristic cuisine. And this to me is the deepest stroke, the unkindest cut, of oppression, especially as it has distorted Black Americans. America, where the suppliant, far from rebelling or even disagreeing with the forces that have caused him to suffer, readily backs them up and finally tries to become an honorary oppressor himself.

No language? No characteristic food? Oh, man, come on.

Maws are things ofays seldom get to peck, nor are you likely ever to hear about Charlie eating a chitterling. Sweet potato pies, a good friend of mine asked recently, "Do they taste anything like pumpkin?" Negative. They taste more like memory, if you're not uptown.

All those different kinds of greens (now quick frozen for anyone) once were all Sam got to eat. (Plus the potlikker, into which one slipped some thrown away meat.) Collards and turnips and kale and mustards were not fit for anybody but the woogies. So they found a way to make them taste like something somebody would want to freeze and sell to a Negro going to Harvard as exotic European spinach.

The watermelon, friend, was imported from Africa (by whom?) where it had been growing many centuries before it was necessary for some people to deny that they had ever tasted one.

Did you ever hear of a black-eyed pea? (Whitey used it for forage, but some folks couldn't.) And all those weird parts of the hog? (After the pig was stripped of its choicest parts, the feet, snout, tail, intestines, stomach, etc., were all left for the "members," who treated them mercilessly.) Is it mere myth that shades are death on chickens? (Deep fat frying, the Dutch found out in 17th century New Amsterdam, was an African speciality: and if you can get hold of a fried chicken leg, or a fried porgie, you can find out what happened to that tradition.)

I had to go to Rutgers before I found people who thought grits were meant to be eaten with milk and sugar, instead of gravy and pork sausage . . . and that's one of the reasons I left.

Away from home, you must make the trip uptown to get really straight as far as a good grease is concerned. People kill chickens all over the world, but chasing them through the dark on somebody else's property would probably insure, once they went in the big bag, that you'd find some really beautiful way to eat them. I mean, after all the risk involved. The fruit of that tradition unfolds everywhere above 100th Street. There are probably more restaurants in Harlem whose staple is fried chicken, or chicken in the basket, than any other place in the world. Ditto, barbecued ribs—also straight out of the South with the West Indians, i.e., Africans from farther south in the West, having developed the best sauce for roasting whole oxen and hogs, spicy and extremely hot.

Hoppin' John (black-eyed peas and rice), hushpuppies (crusty cornmeal bread cooked in fish grease and best with fried fish, especially fried salt fish, which ought to soak overnight unless you're over fifty and can take all that salt), hoecake (pan bread), buttermilk biscuits and pancakes, fatback, *i.e.*, streak'alean-streak'afat, dumplings, neck bones, knuckles (both good for seasoning limas or string beans), okra (another African importation, other name gumbo), pork chops—some more staples of the Harlem cuisine. Most of the food came north when the people did.

There are hundreds of tiny restaurants, food shops, rib joints, shrimp shacks, chicken shacks, "rotisseries" throughout Harlem that serve "soul food"—say, a breakfast of grits, eggs and sausage, pancakes and Alaga syrup—and even tiny booths where it's at least possible to get a good piece of barbecue, hot enough to make you whistle, or a chicken wing on a piece of greasy bread. You can *always* find a fish sandwich: a fish sandwich is something you walk with, or "Two of those small sweet potato pies to go." The Muslim temple serves bean pies which are really separate. It is never necessary to go to some big expensive place to get a good filling grease. You *can* go to the Red Rooster, or Wells, or Joch's, and get a good meal, but Jennylin's, a little place on 135th near Lenox, is more filling, or some place like the A&A food shop in a basement up in the 140's, and you can really get away. I guess a square is somebody who's in Harlem and eats at Nedicks.

the myth of a "negro literature"*

The mediocrity of what has been called "Negro Literature" is one of the most loosely held secrets of American culture. From Phyllis Wheatley to Charles Chesnutt, to the present generation of American Negro writers, the only recognizable accretion of tradition readily attributable to the black producer of a formal literature in this country, with a few notable exceptions, has been of an almost agonizing mediocrity. In most other fields of "high art" in America, with the same few notable exceptions, the Negro contribution has been, when one existed at all, one of impressive mediocrity. Only in music, and most notably in blues, jazz, and spirituals, *i.e.*, "Negro Music," has there been a significantly profound contribution by American Negroes.

There are a great many reasons for the spectacular vapidity of the American Negro's accomplishment in other formal, serious art forms—social, economic, political, etc.—but one of the most persistent and aggravating reasons for the absence of achievement among serious Negro artists, except in Negro music, is that in most cases the Negroes who found themselves in a position to pursue some art, especially the art of literature, have been members of the Negro middle class, a group that has always gone out of its way to cultivate *any* medioc-

* An address given at the American Society for African Culture, March 14, 1962.

rity, as long as that mediocrity was guaranteed to prove to America, and recently to the world at large, that they were not really who they were, *i.e.*, Negroes. Negro music alone, because it drew its strengths and beauties out of the depth of the black man's soul, and because to a large extent its traditions could be carried on by the lowest classes of Negroes, has been able to survive the constant and willful dilutions of the black middle class. Blues and jazz have been the only consistent exhibitors of "Negritude" in formal American culture simply because the bearers of its tradition maintained their essential identities as Negroes; in no other art (and I will persist in calling Negro music, Art) has this been possible. Phyllis Wheatley and her pleasant imitations of 18th century English poetry are far and, finally, ludicrous departures from the huge black voices that splintered Southern nights with their *hollers, chants, arwhoolies,* and *ballits.* The embarrassing and inverted paternalism of Charles Chesnutt and his "refined Afro-American" heroes are far cries from the richness and profundity of the blues. And it is impossible to mention the achievements of the Negro in any area of artistic endeavor with as much significance as in spirituals, blues and jazz. There has never been an equivalent to Duke Ellington or Louis Armstrong in Negro writing, and even the best of contemporary literature written by Negroes cannot yet be compared to the fantastic beauty of the music of Charlie Parker.

American Negro music from its inception moved logically and powerfully out of a fusion between African musical tradition and the American experience. It was, and continues to be, a natural, yet highly stylized and personal version of the Negro's life in America. It is, indeed, a chronicler of the Negro's movement, from African slave to American slave, from Freedman to Citizen. And the literature of the blues is a much more profound contribution to Western culture than any other literary contribution made by American Negroes. Moreover, it is only recently that formal literature written by American Negroes has begun to approach the literary standards of its model, *i.e.*, the literature of the white middle class. And only Jean Toomer, Richard Wright, Ralph Ellison, and James Baldwin have managed to bring off examples of writing, in this genre, that could succeed in passing themselves off as "serious" writing, in the sense that, say, the work of Somerset Maugham is "serious" writing. That is, serious, if one has never read Herman Melville or James Joyce. And it is part of the tragic naïveté of the middle-class (brow) writer, that he has not.

Literature, for the Negro writer, was always an example of "culture." Not in the sense of the more impressive philosophical characteristics of a particular social group, but in the narrow sense of "cultivation" or "sophistication" by an individual within that group. The Negro artist, because of his middle-class background, carried the artificial social burden as the "best and most intelligent" of Negroes, and usually entered into the "serious" arts to exhibit his familiarity with the social graces, *i.e.*, as a method or means of displaying his participation in the "serious" aspects of American culture. To be a writer was to be "cultivated," in the stunted bourgeois sense of the word. It was also to be a "quality" black man. It had nothing to do with the investigation of the human soul. It was, and is, a social preoccupation rather than an aesthetic one. A rather daring way of status seeking.

The cultivated Negro leaving those ineffectual philanthropies, Negro colleges, looked at literature merely as another way of gaining prestige in the white world for the Negro middle class. And the literary and artistic models were always those that could be socially acceptable to the white middle class, which automatically limited them to the most spiritually debilitated imitations of literature available. Negro music, to the middle class, black and white, was never socially acceptable. It was shunned by blacks ambitious of "waking up white," as low and degrading. It was shunned by their white models simply because it was produced by blacks. As one of my professors at Howard University protested one day, "It's amazing how much bad taste the blues display." Suffice it to say, it is in part exactly this "bad taste" that has continued to keep Negro music as vital as it is. The abandonment of one's local (*i.e.*, place or group) emotional attachments in favor of the abstract emotional response of what is called "the general public" (which is notoriously white and middle class) has always been the great diluter of any Negro culture. "You're acting like a nigger," was the standard disparagement. I remember being chastised severely for daring to eat a piece of watermelon on the Howard campus. "Do you realize you're sitting near the highway?" is what the man said. "This is the capstone of Negro education." And it is too, in the sense that it teaches the Negro how to make out in the white society, using the agonizing overcompensation of pretending he's also white. James Baldwin's play, *The Amen Corner*, when it appeared at the Howard Players theatre, "set the speech department back ten years," an English professor groaned to me. The play depicted the lives of poor Negroes running a store-front church. Any reference to the Negro-ness of the American Negro has always been frowned upon by the black middle class in their frenzied dash toward the precipice of the American mainstream.

High art, first of all, must reflect the experiences of the human being, the emotional predicament of the man, as he exists, in the defined world of his being. It must be produced from the legitimate emotional resources of the soul in the world. It can *never* be produced by evading these resources or pretending that they do not exist. It can never be produced by appropriating the withered emotional responses of some strictly social idea of humanity. High art, and by this I mean any art that would attempt to describe or characterize some portion of the profound meaningfulness of human life with any finality or truth, cannot be based on the superficialities of human existence. It must issue from *real* categories of human activity, *truthful* accounts of human life, and not fancied accounts of the attainment of cultural privilege by some willingly preposterous apologists for one social "order" or another. Most of the formal literature produced by Negroes in America has never fulfilled these conditions. And aside from Negro music, it is only in the "popular traditions" of the so-called lower-class Negro that these conditions are fulfilled as a basis for human life. And it is because of this "separation" between Negro life (as an emotional experience) and Negro art, that, say, Jack Johnson or Ray Robinson is a larger cultural hero than any Negro writer. It is because of this separation, even evasion, of the emotional experience of Negro life, that Jack Johnson is a more modern political symbol than most Negro writers. Johnson's life, as proposed, certainly, by his career, reflects much more accurately the symbolic yearnings for singular values among the great masses of Negroes than any black novelist has yet managed to convey. Where is the Negro-ness of a literature written in imitation of the meanest of social intelligences to be found in American culture, *i.e.*, the white middle class? How can it even begin to express the emotional predicament of black Western man? Such a literature, even if its "characters" *are* black, takes on the emotional barrenness of its model, and the blackness of the characters is like the blackness of Al Jolson, an unconvincing device. It is like using black checkers instead of white. They are still checkers.

The development of the Negro's music was, as I said, direct and instinctive. It was the one vector out of African culture impossible to eradicate completely. The appearance of blues as a native *American* music signified in many ways the appearance of American Negroes where once there were African Negroes. The emotional fabric of the music was colored by the emergence of an American Negro culture. It signified that culture's strength and vitality. In the evolution of form in Negro music it is possible to see not only the evolution of the Negro as a cultural and social element of American culture, but also the evolution of that culture itself. The "Coon Shout" proposed one version of the American Negro—and of America; Ornette Coleman proposes another. But the point is that both these versions are accurate and informed with a legitimacy of emotional concern nowhere available in what is called "Negro Literature," and certainly not in the middlebrow literature of the white American.

The artifacts of African art and sculpture were consciously eradicated by slavery. Any African art that based its validity on the production of an artifact, *i.e.*, some *material* manifestation such as a wooden statue or a woven cloth, had little chance of survival. It was only the more "abstract" aspects of African culture that could continue to exist in slave America. Africanisms still persist in the music, religion, and popular cultural traditions of American Negroes. However, it is not an African art American Negroes are responsible for, but an American one. The traditions of Africa must be utilized within the culture of the American Negro where they *actually* exist, and not because of a defensive rationalization about the *worth* of one's ancestors or an attempt to capitalize on the recent eminence of the "new" African nations. Africanisms do exist in Negro culture, but they have been so translated and transmuted by the American experience that they have become integral parts of that experience.

The American Negro has a definable and legitimate historical tradition, no matter how painful, in America, but it is the only place such a tradition exists, simply because America is the only place the American Negro exists. He is, as William Carlos Williams said, "A pure product of America." The paradox of the Negro experience in America is that it is a separate experience, but inseparable from the complete fabric of American life. The history of Western culture begins for the Negro with the importation of the slaves. It is almost as if all Western history before that must be strictly a learned concept. It is only the American experience that can be a persistent cultural catalyst for the Negro. In a sense, history for the Negro, before America, must remain an emotional abstraction. The cultural memory of Africa informs the Negro's life in America, but it is impossible to separate it from its American transformation. Thus, the Negro writer, if he wanted to tap his legitimate cultural tradition, should have done it by utilizing the entire spectrum of the American experience from the point of view of the emotional history of the black man in this country: as its victim and its chronicler. The soul of such a man, as it exists outside the boundaries of commercial diversion or artificial social pretense. But without a deep commitment to cultural relevance and intellectual purity this was impossible. The Negro, as a writer, was always a social object, whether glorifying the concept of white superiority, as a great many early Negro writers did, or in crying out against it, as exemplified by the stock "protest" literature of the thirties. He never moved into the position where he could propose his own symbols, erect his own personal myths, as any great literature must. Negro writing was always "after the fact," *i.e.*, based on known social concepts within the structure of bourgeois idealistic projections of "their America," and an emotional climate that never really existed.

The most successful fiction of most Negro writing is in its emotional content. The Negro protest novelist postures, and invents a protest quite amenable with the tradition of bourgeois American life. He never reaches the central core of the America which *can* cause such protest. The intellectual traditions of the white middle class prevent such exposure of reality, and the black imitators reflect this. The Negro writer on Negro life in America postures, and invents a Negro life, and an America to contain it. And even most of those who tried to rebel against that *invented* America were trapped because they had lost all touch with the reality of their experience within the *real* America, either because of the hidden emotional allegiance to the white middle class, or because they did not realize where the reality of their experience lay. When the serious Negro writer disdained the "middlebrow" model, as is the case with a few contemporary black American writers, he usually rushed headlong into the groves of the Academy, perhaps the most insidious and clever dispenser of middlebrow standards of excellence under the guise of "recognizable tradition." That such recognizable tradition is necessary goes without saying, but even from the great philosophies of Europe a contemporary usage must be established. No poetry has come out of England of major importance for forty years, yet there are would-be Negro poets who reject the gaudy excellence of 20th century American poetry in favor of disembowelled academic models of second-rate English poetry, with the notion that somehow it is the only way poetry should be written. It would be better if such a poet listened to Bessie Smith sing "Gimme a Pigfoot," or listened to the tragic verse of a Billie Holiday, than be content to imperfectly imitate the bad poetry of the ruined minds of Europe. And again, it is this striving for *respectability* that has it so. For an American, black or white, to say that some hideous imitation of Alexander Pope means more to him, emotionally, than the blues of Ray Charles or Lightnin' Hopkins, it would be required for him to have completely disappeared into the American Academy's vision of a Europeanized and colonial American culture, or to be lying. In the end, the same emotional sterility results. It is somehow much more tragic for the black man.

A Negro literature, to be a legitimate product of the Negro experience in America, must get at that experience in exactly the terms America has proposed for it, in its most ruthless identity. Negro reaction to America is as deep a part of America as the root causes of that reaction, and it is impossible to accurately describe that reaction in terms of the American middle class; because for them, the Negro has never really existed, never been glimpsed in anything even approaching the complete reality of his humanity. The Negro writer has to go from where he actually is, completely outside of that conscious white myopia. That the Negro does exist is the point, and as an element of American culture he is completely misunderstood by Americans. The middlebrow, commercial Negro writer assures the white American that, in fact, he doesn't exist, and that if he does, he does so within the perfectly predictable fingerpainting of white bourgeois sentiment and understanding. Nothing could be further from the truth. The Creoles of New Orleans resisted "Negro" music for a time as raw and raucous, because they thought they had found a place within the white society which would preclude their being Negroes. But they were unsuccessful in their attempts to "disappear" because the whites themselves reminded them that they were still, for all their assimilation, "just coons." And this seems to me an extremely important idea, since it is precisely this bitter insistence that has kept what can be called "Negro Culture" a brilliant amalgam of diverse influences. There was always a border beyond which the Negro could not go, whether

musically or socially. There was always a possible limi-
tation to any dilution or excess of cultural or spiritual
reference. The Negro could not ever become white and
that was his strength; at some point, always, he could
not participate in the dominant tenor of the white man's
culture, yet he came to understand that culture as well
as the white man. It was at this juncture that he had
to make use of other resources, whether African, sub-
cultural, or hermetic. And it was this boundary, this no-
man's-land, that provided the logic and beauty of his
music. And this is the only way for the Negro artist to
provide his version of America—from that no-man's-
land outside the mainstream. A no-man's-land, a black
country, completely invisible to white America, but so
essentially part of it as to stain its whole being an omi-
nous gray. Were there really a Negro literature, now it
could flower. At this point when the whole of Western
society might go up in flames, the Negro remains an integral part of that society, but continually outside it, a
figure like Melville's Bartleby. He is an American, capable of identifying emotionally with the fantastic cultural ingredients of this society, but he is also, forever,
outside that culture, an invisible strength within it, an
observer. If there is ever a Negro literature, it must dis-
engage itself from the weak, heinous elements of the
culture that spawned it, and use its very existence as
evidence of a more profound America. But as long as
the Negro writer contents himself with the imitation of
the useless ugly inelegance of the stunted middle-class
mind, academic or popular, and refuses to look around
him and "tell it like it is"—preferring the false prestige
of the black bourgeosie or the deceitful "acceptance" of

buy and sell America, something never included in the legitimate cultural tradition of "his people"—he will be a
failure, and what is worse, not even a significant failure.
Just another dead American.

1963

brief reflections on two hot shots

Where a great deal of public "sophistication" is allowed among oppressed people, the stupid misunderstanding can very quickly arise that one of them may be an "individual." This is perhaps James Baldwin's favorite word. A man like Peter Abrahams, the South African writer, also is given to using this word, as if it really meant something or could describe some actual quality in his life. But the interesting fact is, I think, that even Abrahams' overly passionate declaration of "individuality" (*e.g.*, when faced with the decision of whether to stay with Jomo Kenyatta for a weekend or at a hotel which the British Government would provide: "It dawned on me that I had become, for the moment, the battlefield of that horrible animal, the racial struggle. I made up my mind, resenting both sides . . .") is made—out Baldwinning James with the plea for understanding as an individual, a separate entity—*only* by virtue of his own claim. Earlier Mr. Abrahams spoke of the horror in South Africa as "the ugly war of color," and the idea of "the racial struggle" as "that horrible animal" curdles the blood when you realize it is coming from a black man, and not the innocent white liberal made fierce by homosexuality. Again the *cry*, the spavined whine and plea of these Baldwins and Abrahams, is sickening past belief. Why should anyone think of these men as individuals? Merely because they are able to shriek the shriek of a fashionable international body of white middle-class society? Joan of Arc of the cocktail party is what is being presented through the writings and postures of men like these. As if the highest form of compliment the missionaries could receive was to see their boys making good, On Their Own, rattling off sensitivity ratios at parties. As if "I am sensitive too" was the final statement man makes before the final decision to enter into the covenant of intelligent life. Swaggering peers of peace.

But individuality is not merely the cross one select number willfully bears among the broken heads and lives of the oppressed. We need not call to each other through the flames if we have nothing to say, or are merely diminishing the history of the world with descriptions of it that will show we are intelligent. Intelligence is only valuable when it is contained naturally in the matter we present as a result of the act (of writing . . . of feeling). A writer is committed to what is real and not to the sanctity of his FEELINGS. So that Abrahams and Baldwin want the hopeless filth of enforced ignorance to be stopped only because they are sometimes confused with the sufferers. They are too hip to be *real* black men, for instance—this is only, let us say, a covering to register their feelings, a gay exotic plumage as they dissemble in the world of ideas, and always come home with the shaky ones.

If one has nothing TO SAY but, "I can feel," or, "I am intelligent," there is really no need saying it. These things in themselves are very boring. So many people are intelligent and, you bet, sensitive. Unless a man will tell you something, pass on some piece of information about the world, and by so doing show you that part of the world he moves in, there is little value in what he is saying. It is like a high diver perfecting all his moves in the house. He *must* get out there and jump off that board before anything happens. I would not pay to see an acrobat slide off the commode.

Finally it is deadly simple. A writer must have a point of view, or he cannot be a good writer. He must be standing somewhere in the world, or else he is not one of *us*, and his commentary then is of little value. But even air is warmed by the sun. How can a man escape?

Individuality is only gained by first realizing that it is not important in its most superficial states. The quality of an idea (or life) makes it singular: what it is about. An idea must be specific and useful, and must function in the world; it must be, even, an interpretation of that world that permits a man to use himself. The singular man uses, first, himself. That is why he is singular. Because few do.

Being a writer does not necessarily mean that a man will be singular. There are more bad writers than bad atomic scientists. Being sensitive means primarily that you do not like to see lynchings. But the vacuum behind such a circumstance can be, and usually is, immense. Men like Baldwin and Abrahams want to live free from such "ugly" things as "the racial struggle" because (they imply) they simply cannot stand what it does to men.

FACT: There is a racial struggle.
FACT: Any man had better realize what it means. Why there is one. It is the result of *more* than "misunderstanding." Money is not simply something one gets for publishing novels or selling paintings.
FACT: "People should love each other" sounds like Riis Park at sundown. It has very little meaning to the world at large.

In terms of the racial struggle, the only "individuals" would be people who did not have to worry about it. I have to worry about the racial struggle. If Abrahams and Baldwin try to forget about it, and be individuals, some gruff realist brings them back, usually with one not even carefully chosen word or phrase. That is a very shaky individuality to my mind. Where I am most singular, in the taking hold of material presented me each second by the world, there is not the least chance that one word is going to throw me back and into some chattery panic. But knowing what is the world's and what is your own is to me a very priceless and basic knowledge. You cannot make it unless you do. Valuable energies are wasted otherwise.

My faith in Melville, for instance, and the faith I give his language, is completely passed through the world into my own references of mind and spirit. They cannot be got at. But I work with street people on picketing and lecturing poor, ignorant Negroes because that work is not only necessary, but open to any interpretation. It passes too, beyond results, to where I feel the use of anything. You cannot tell me what I mean by Socialism. Only I can tell you. But I can tell you what Mr. Abrahams means, and what Mr. Baldwin means, and they will not even open their mouths to say anything but that they are well-dressed, educated and have feelings that are easily hurt. They are telling us that this is no world for hedonists in the iron maiden factory, where they have been forced to live. About whom they think is making these heavy ladies, they grow more vague, and look languidly out the window toward the windy lake of pure social commerce. As Abrahams says, "When I had left South Africa in the dim and distant past, there were isolated islands where black and white could meet in neutral territory." Those islands floating happily in the sun. In a sky unblemished by the awkward goons of information. In their anger and boredom the writers begin to do a little dance. It is known as *The Martyrs' Shuffle*, in cocktail time. Won't somebody please help them move?

Deadly simple. If Abrahams and Baldwin were turned white, for example, there would be no more noise from them. Not because they consciously desire that, but because then they could be sensitive in peace. Their color is the only obstruction I can see to this state they seek, and I see no reason they should be denied it for so paltry a thing as heavy pigmentation. Somebody turn them! And then perhaps the rest of us can get down to the work at hand. Cutting throats!

a dark bag

This review or chronicle might be my last liberal, or non-literal, act, unless quite soon there bursts within me an enormous gland of misplaced and not wholly unsentimental regard for the social malaise that so willingly shapes (and has for the last thirty years shaped) the flexibly official political/cultural tone of this society's complete retreat into fantasy and self-destruction. I mean I hope it is my last personal gesture of "adjustment" in the direction of a burning building. (My last previous gesture was to place two bets on Floyd Patterson.) So let this also serve as a loud cry for the firemen, or whatever other realists there may be in the area. Possibly only the fire is real.

All the books mentioned in this chronicle focus on the writings of black men, in one part of the world or another. That is the reason they are gathered together here, as a chronicle review. If there is any other reason in God's (or whoever's) universe why these books are here, or for that matter if there is any other reason any reader can think of, may he speak quite soon, or cede the point.

In such a gathering, unless one has special vested emotional interests in hoping for something different, as I admittedly have, there is usually not much hope of running into anything of a strictly literary persuasion.

We can be pretty certain when faced with a batch of books by black men, *anywhere*, of being told quite a few definite truths, a great many of which we must already be familiar with if we are vulgar enough to be "modern" people, and not fools, or Madox Ford Anglicans.

For instance, in each of the three anthologies listed here one will find poems that tell us the black man has been oppressed and generally misused, usually by the white man. Very few of these poems, however, tell us what that is like, at least very few do with even the intensity of Kipling telling us what it is like to do the oppressing, or know people that do. And in such cases, where what we are faced with is the *act* of "protest," certainly a picket sign, or a pistol, would do much more good. Unless we wanted to have very cultivated picket signs that began, "O, White Man," or more exactly (from Melvin Tolson's "Dark Symphony" published in *American Negro Poetry**), "Oh, how can we forget/Our human rights denied?/Oh, how can we forget/Our manhood crucified?" Walk quietly and carry big signs.

I mean there is no point in this being poetry, *especially*. No poetic point has been made, though granted the moral fact is clear enough before the writing. So clear in fact that editors of literary magazines find room from time to time to publish or review such work as a gesture in the direction of flashy moral presumption. But, unfortunately, it is usually like listening to muffled sounds in a closet. And, right! If we open the door, they might be ghosts.

I have said elsewhere (*Saturday Review*) that I think the reason there have not been a great many interesting

---

* *American Negro Poetry*, Arna Bontemps, editor (Hill and Wang, 1963).

Negro writers (in the United States) is that most of the Negroes who've found themselves in a position to become writers were middle-class Negroes who thought of literature as a way of proving they were not "inferior" (and quite a few who wanted to prove that they were). Negro music does not suffer generally from such pathology, to show a specific contrast, simply because most of the great Negro musicians never felt the need to show anything in their playing but the power of their insights. And one can find more moving writing in any of Chester Himes' bizarre detective novels than in most more "serious" efforts by Negroes, just because Himes' main interest must be in saying the thing like it is. For instance, part of every English sentence James Baldwin writes must be given over to telling a willing audience how sensitive and intelligent he is, in the face of terrible odds. Ralph Ellison's extra-literary commercial is usually about European literature, the fact that he has done some reading in it. These weights extend throughout what is called Negro Literature: in the nineteenth century Charles Chesnutt's nonliterary burden was that he was "a refined Afro-American."

But let there be no misunderstanding. I do believe, desperately, in a "poetry of ideas." Poems have got, literally, to be about something. And the weights of love, murder, history, economics, etc., have got to drag whoever's writing in a personally sanctified direction or there will be no poems at all. But it is not the direction that's interesting, or makes literature or art, but the replaying of it by the poet. All of my work, for instance, is written by a Negro writer. If I say, "Look at that woman falling out of the window," it is a Negro who is saying it. And whether I say, "Listen, it is a Negro saying, look at that woman, etc.," or not, the fact remains that a Negro has said it. And that fact should *somehow* inform the telling. The point, of course, is *how* should it inform? And my answer is that it should inform through the intensity of personal response and the uniqueness of private emotional concern. A poet writing a poem about the black man being oppressed by the white must keep that concern *within* the poem. Otherwise there will form a hard-shell of talk and opinion around what the poet thinks he is saying, and the matter should be lost like the newspapers.

But we must work with what we have. From wherever in the landscape. (One speaks of the Russian soul of Dostoevsky, the *canto hondo* and Spanishness of Lorca, the French genius of Molière.) We are stung by some things in our lives that must tell who we are, almost as specifically as on our driver's license. They comprise an effortless power readily at our use, if we can find an effective method. Which is what I mean if I ever say the word "technique"; how to effectively express what we know.

It cannot be, as Gregory Corso said recently of black writers, "They fail because they are stuck with talking about their people." (But then G.C., I think, will never understand that despite a little evidence to the contrary, he will always address whomever he does address in the world through his poems as the inspired scion of immigrant Italians, whether he chooses to use this fact concretely as working matter within the poems, or merely, like so many others, as an exotic portmanteau of labored sensitivity. Like the man I know who has changed his nose and name but still speaks lovingly of *Jews*.) If Whitman and W. C. Williams were not talking about "their people," what in Christ's name were they talking about? It is the *how* that is, and will remain, important. And, happily, some of the authors included in the collections I will mention here have been aware of this fact.

Anthologies are usually taste-manuals, fashion reinforcers, or, at best, reflections of the editor's personality and total grasp of his material. *American Negro Poetry*, edited by Arna Bontemps, falls very quickly into the last category, and the anthology is a grab bag of pretense and amateurish misunderstanding, in much the same way that most anthologies of Negro writing have usually been. And this has been the case not only because, as I mentioned, there has not been overly much to anthologize, but also because the anthologists have been the world's worst. I suppose because the subject just didn't seem interesting enough. Mr. Bontemps easily continues this tradition simply because, as far as I can see from the tasteless breadth of his selection (which includes historical fiction writer Frank Yerby—of whom Mr. Bontemps seems genuinely proud, I would suppose because he is a rich black man—and other names who seem by the cast of their work to be sweet soul sisters and brothers who write poems every time something makes them happy) and an amazingly noncritical selection of the material included by each poet, he does not know too much about any poetry, black, white, or yellow. But even so, there are a few poets in the book and a few lines that should have been spared this immersion in another house slave's manual of verse.

Jean Toomer, for instance, whose work, though mightily uneven and often dimmed by a too close association with the elastic phrases of Hart Crane, still ought to be better known. He was capable of producing gorgeous lines like, "Pour O pour that parting soul in song,/O pour it in the saw-dust glow of night,/Into the velvet pine-smoke air tonight,/And let the valley carry it along./And let the valley carry it along."

There is, of course, some other work in this volume too. The James Weldon Johnson, Paul Laurence Dunbar, Claude McKay, Countee Cullen, etc., selections are in as expected. There are thirteen poems by Langston Hughes, including early ones I've always liked, "The Negro Speaks Of Rivers" and "Dream Variation," but most of the poems are simply not good. (There are only three of Toomer's poems included.) Richard Wright has a very eerie poem about a lynching that is worth most of the other material in the anthology, and eight lovely, though overly literary, haiku. Robert Hayden's poems, as self-consciously big-wordy as they are, are still full of wild-dream renderings in water-tight rhythms that need a fuller audience. Gwendolyn Brooks, the Pulitzer Prize winner, who is capable of a lyrical preciseness like, "The blowing of clear wind in your gay hair;/Love changeful in you (like a music, or/Like a sweet mournfulness, or like a dance,/Or like the tender struggle of a fan)," is also capable, under Mr. Bontemps' permissive editorial hand, of dumbness like, "The loveliest lynchee was our Lord."

M. Carl Holman, Russell Atkins, Conrad Kent Rivers, and some others also present work of actual literary merit, which is, you bet, very cool praise. (And there are a few very interesting younger Negro poets not included in this book whose work would have certainly lifted the quality of the volume, *e.g.*, A. B. Spellman, Lorenzo Thomas, Bob Kaufman, Joe Johnson, Allen Polite, to name quickly some I know.)

Langston Hughes' anthology *Poems From Black Africa** suffers from the same kind of anemia as Mr. Bontemps', with the added frustration of generally hopeless translations. But this is a very useful book, if only because there are so few volumes of African poetry available in English, or for that matter in the original languages, in this country.

Again, Mr. Hughes' editorial hand is generally unsteady, and while he is certainly more knowledgeable about poetry and about the intent of his anthology than Mr. Bontemps, it is still difficult to understand why he included some of the poets at all, if his selections are truly representative of their work.

One striking fact was that very generally speaking there seems to be a much better quality of poetry being written by Africans (and West Indians) in French than in English. Although John Pepper Clark, Christopher Okigbo, and Ezekiel Mphahlele, who is also a very fine essayist, write a strong, more than "interesting" kind of poetry in English, French-speaking writers like Jean-Joseph Ravearivelo from Madagascar and, predictably, Léopold Sédar-Senghor, the President of Senegal, and Alioune Diop, both already possessing some small measure of fame in this country, seem the most powerful writers on the continent, even in the face of the most sinister translations I've ever encountered. (There are

---

* *Poems From Black Africa*, Langston Hughes, editor (Indiana University Press, 1963).

two other black French writers, though not Africans, whose work I value, Leon Damas of French Guiana and Aimé Césaire of Martinique, whose work should have been brought out in English years ago.)

Almost all the African poets writing in English included in this collection, with the general exception of the writers I mentioned—and their work is not entirely free of it—employ the meta-language and shallow ornament of contemporary academic British poetry with, a great deal of the time, the same dreary results. Heath-Stubbs, Larkin, Hamburger, etc., are paraded through much English-African poetry—possibly this imitation is just a clinging residue of Victorianism and another middle class's idea of literary respectability. And the poetry reflects, especially in its use of very literary African Environmental Images, the true missionaries' legacy of exchanging the Big Letter God for the many small letter ones. (As Michael Dei-Anang of Ghana writes, "Who nursed the doubtful child/Of civilization/On the wand'ring banks/Of the life-giving Nile,/And gave to the teeming nations/Of the West a Grecian gift.") It is flat-footed and free of intellectual grace, because of its overly literal, defensive stance, as well as the hopelessly rhetorical language which is as missionary-tainted as Mr. Nkrumah's navy blue suits. But even so, many times these poems *seem* interesting for a time, if only because of the bright, sometimes exotic, backgrounds and references. (This is one marked advantage over contemporary British poetry.)

John Pepper Clark, in the few poems he has in the Hughes anthology, but more so because of his verse play *Song of a Goat*, convinces me that he is one of the most interesting Africans writing, English or French. Mr. Clark is a Nigerian, born in 1935, though I understand he is now in the graduate school at Princeton. For sure, nothing he could ever learn at Princeton would help him write so beautiful a work as *Song of a Goat*.* It is English, but it is not. The tone, the references (immediate and accreted) belong to what I must consider an African experience. The English is pushed, as Senghor wished all Africans to do with European languages, past the immaculate boredom of the recent Victorians to a quality of experience that is non-European, though it is the European tongue which seems to shape it externally. But Clark is after a specific emotional texture nowhere available in European literature or life.

> Masseur: Your womb
> Is open and warm as a room
> It ought to accommodate many.
>
> Ebiere: Well, it seems to like staying empty.
>
> Masseur: An empty house, my daughter, is a thing
> Of danger. If men will not live in it
> Bats or grass will, and that is enough
> Signal for worse things to come in.

The play is about a traditional West African family split and destroyed by adultery. And the writing moves easily through the myth heart of African life, building a kind of ritual drama that depends as much on the writer's insides for its exactness and strength as it does on the narrating of formal ritualistic acts. The language is gentle and lyrical most of the time, but Clark's images and metaphors are strikingly and, I think, indigenously vivid, enabling lines like:

* *Song of a Goat*, John Pepper Clark (Northwestern University Press, 1963).

1st Neighbour: It should be easy to see a leopard
                        If he were here. His eyes should be
                        Blazing forth in the dark.

3rd Neighbour: So I hear. I have heard them likened
                        To the lighthouse out on the bar.

2nd Neighbour: And its motion is silent as that big house
                        We must be careful.

These are African lines, in tone and reference, securing for any reader a sense of "place," and in this sense Senghor's ideas of Negritude become easier to work with. The image of the leopard, that "its motion is silent as that big house," must be African. Houses in Africa—not those of the European variety—do sway gently in any breeze, if they are huts. The most powerful way to deal with an image is to make sure it goes deeper than literature. That it is actually "out there."

Christopher Okigbo's *Heavensgate** is much more "literary" than Mr. Clark's work. And it suffers from that quality, which seems to make it less an extension of Mr. Okigbo qua himself than it is a reflection of an ambitious social/aesthetic program. But he is frequently a moving writer and does, I feel, understand to a large extent how a non-European ought to deal with a European tongue (which is his own). But at this moment, Mr. Okigbo's reading is weakening most of his poems. "Bird of the sun on tree top sitting/on fig tree top mourns under the lamp:/ *etru bo pi alo a she e anando we aquandem* . . ./And when we were great boys/hiding at the smithies/we sang words after the bird-/*kratosbiate* . . ." The echo is unmistakable.

---

* *Heavensgate*, Christopher Okigbo (Northwestern University Press, 1963).

I spoke of the strength of the French-Negro poets, whether in Africa or the West Indies. Leon Damas with his *African Songs** and Jean-Joseph Rabearivelo's *24 Poems*** demonstrate this very elegantly. Mr. Damas' book is, in fact, one of the loveliest things I've come upon in some time. These are literally poems to be sung, and very strongly influenced by traditional African communal and dramatic song form. This is from "Cuckold Contented," which I wish I could quote in its entirety: "I could have certainly/Certainly killed him/If he would not just in time/Just in time have awoken/Just to give me/To give me five pounds/Five pounds which I took/And taking back with me/Taking back with me my wife/Because water takes off the scent/The scent of love/And money doesn't smell/And money smells of nothing."

Rabearivelo's work is delicately surreal, and in that term more determinedly "modern." For example, "The cocks/with their coops pierced by stars/and the other spears of darkness." The poetry is weaker when M. Rabearivelo, like Mr. Okigbo, sacrifices what is strongest and easiest for the artificial badge of French genius and becomes modern or fashionable (in one narrow sphere) at the cost of his own singular understanding of what the world is. The surrealism Senghor and Césaire asked for from the French Negro poets was a more dramatically African use of French, which they thought should be in defiance of European rationalism and not merely thin replicas of Breton or Tzara.

One of the best things about Jacob Drachler's *African*

---

* *African Songs of Love, War, Grief and Abuse*, Leon Damas (Northwestern University Press, 1963).
** *24 Poems*, Jean-Joseph Rabearivelo (Northwestern University Press, 1963).

Heritage,* a generally weak willed collection of prose and poetry by and about Africans, was that it included two articles ("The Black Poet's Search For Identity" by Samuel W. Allen and "The African Renaissance" by Thomas L. Hodgkin) which were full of information about people like Senghor and Césaire, clarifying to some extent their concept of Negritude. This idea seems to me merely a useful, though ironically Classical, statement that reference determines value, and that for every culture there is a definite set of aesthetic, moral, etc., judgments based quite literally on specifically indigenous emotional and psychological response; although it is usually made to seem by European commentators like the crafts program of the Black Muslims.

There are a few other things in this book which are worthwhile as well: Melville Herskovits' article, "Creative Impulses In Dahomean Poetry"; Ezekiel Mphahlele's fragment, "Epilogue To Apartheid"; parts of three badly translated poems of Senghor's; and a few things that managed to get through in Césaire's, *e.g.*, "Peasant may there emerge from the mountain's head she/who wounds the wind/may there cool in her throat a draught of bells . . ."

Lyndon Harries' *Swahili Poetry*** is primarily, I imagine, to be used as an academic guidebook to the amusements of one of the subject peoples. But intent aside, the book is still useful and provides a valuable introduction to a kind of Arab-African poetry, though it does not cover any Swahili poetry written after the nineteenth century, and the tone of its general presentation may be summed up by the author's remark that, "From

---

* *African Heritage*, Jacob Drachler, editor (Crowell-Collier, 1963).
** *Swahili Poetry*, Lyndon Harries (Oxford University Press, 1963).

the amalgam of two traditions we find in Swahili poetry a positive contribution to literature." How very strange.

what does nonviolence mean?

There is a war going on now in the United States. Anyone who does not understand how this could be possible is more naïve, fortunately or unfortunately, than one would think this century would permit.

Recently in that war, four Negro children were blown to bits while they were learning to pray. The leader of the Jackson, Mississippi, NAACP (himself a reluctant convert to "the doctrines of nonviolence") was assassinated in front of his home. Police dogs, fire hoses, blackjacks, have been used on Negroes, trying to reinforce a simple and brutal social repression. And all these terroristic tactics are used, finally, toward the same end: to make young bucks and tottering school marms confess to the same lie the racks and iron maidens of the Inquisition demanded—that there is something other than reality. While a Negro is under a hose or thrown against a building by some dumb brute, he is supporting that lie as well as the lie of his own inferiority. The inferiority of the suppliant. The readiness of the weak to repeat themselves. To be no more than weak, or no smarter than their torturers. Yet in spite of this, and in the face of such brutality, certain elements in America ask the Negro to be Nonviolent. But who are these elements, and what are they really asking?

On all levels the white man insists that there is no

Negro in America like the one that claims now to be here. Or at least there has been a constant and unfailing effort on the part of almost every white man in America (and the West) to have his own qualified version of a black man exist, and not just any black man who might like to appear under his own volition. To the Southern white (and many Northerners) the sit-ins are liars, the pickets and boycotters, all are fiendish liars. There is no such Negro who would want anything but what we've always given them, the white Southerner says. The Negro who wants the foot off his neck must be inspired by Communists. It is a simple lie to say otherwise, they say. We know what Negroes are, what they want. Governor Wallace, on television, admonishes his black housekeeper warmly, "Y'all take care of everything, heah?" The old woman smiles, and goes off to take care of his baby. That is the Negro that really exists for him. No other. The smiling convicts raking up leaves in his yard. He waves as he crosses to his car. More real Negroes. He is on his way to the University to make the fake Negroes disappear.

The liberal white man insists also that there is no such thing as a Negro, except the thing he has invented. They are simply underprivileged, the have-nots, the emerging. They are the same as we, given an education, a livelihood, etc. And this is the rhetoric. But where did all these underprivileged people, these have-nots, come from? What, for instance, are all these black people doing in this country in the first place? It is questions like these that the rhetoric is supposed to erase from the liberal white man's mind. The fact that the Negro was brought here as an African slave, and that he labored some two hundred years in slavery, is by now supposedly forgotten. (During slavery a liberal, or a moderate, was a man who didn't want the slaves beaten. But he was not asking that they be freed.) Certainly the Negro middle class has forgotten, or at least it is their job to pretend they have forgotten, and for this reason even the low moan of blues from some un-American tenement is almost as much of a social affront as a sign on a water fountain. This is the missionaries' legacy, the last pure remnant of the slave mentality—cultural shame.

What the liberal white man does is to open a door into the glittering mainstream of white American life as a possibility for the middle-class black man. All the Negro need do is renounce his history as pure social error and strive with the rest of the strivers, so that he too can help in erecting a monolithic syndrome of predictable social values, based on the economic power and hegemony of the American (Western) white man.

In order for the Negro to achieve what I will call an "equality of means," that is, at birth to be able to benefit by everything of value in the society, of course the society would have to change almost completely. What the liberal white man wants is to change the Negro so he can be included in the existing system. Richard Nixon is an example of what the liberal wants the Negro to become. A drab lower middle-class buffoon who has no more political power or cultural significance than his social interment petty ambition allows. Very few American white men want the system itself changed, and that change complete, or occurring with the rudeness of sudden reality. Abracadabra, a family of twelve Negroes is living in the next lot. What shall we do? the cry goes up from the kindest hearts.

It is the same kind of spurious and pragmatic realism that motivates most American "reformers," e.g., most of the socio-economic policies of Roosevelt's New Deal were not meant to change the society, but to strengthen the one that existed. Roosevelt, in this sense, like a man who when fire breaks out in his apartment immediately builds a stove around it, gave a flexibility to the American ruling class that it could not have survived without.

So far the most serious battles in the war I spoke of are being waged between two classes of white men, although the middle-class Negroes are the semi-conscious pawns in these struggles. (The rest of the black population are pawns by default.) The battles are being waged now, have been waged for the last three hundred years, between those white men who think the Negro is good for one thing and those who think he is good for another. This same fight went on during the early days of slavery between the missionaries, those who would give the slave Christianity, thereby excusing the instance of slavery as a moral crusade (with concomitant economic advantages) and those who felt that as animals the black men had no need for God, since as animals they had no souls. The fight continues today, with the same emphasis. Except in earlier times the liberal forces, the God-carriers, had only the house slave, or occasional freedman, to show off as end products of a benevolent Christian ethic, but now the Kennedys and the Rockefellers have a full-fledged black bourgeoisie to gesture toward as an indication of what the social utopia of the West should look like.

So the war goes on, from battle to battle, but with essentially the same things at stake, and for the same reasons. The forces of naked repression, on the one hand, have always been out in the open. What they want, have wanted, is common knowledge to Negroes once Negroes have gotten old enough to find out that the world as they will come to know it is basically unfriendly if you are black. Each "class" (of white people) has its own method of making that world unfriendly, which makes the quarrel. But nothing is really to be changed. Complete socio-economic subjugation is the goal of both white forces. What the liberal sees as evil about this program is the way it is being carried out. Liberals want to be leaders rather than rulers.

The black middle class, and its spiritual forebears, the freedmen and house slaves, have always "fought" to maintain some hegemony and privilege, and as a privileged class within the American system as defined by the Liberal/Missionary class of American white men. And because of this they have always had to be pawns and tokens in the white class war that constantly goes on over the question of what to do with Negroes. The NAACP, SCLC, CORE, and any other group who advocate moral suasion as their weapon of change (reform) have been members of the Negro middle class, or at least bound by that class's social sentiments. These organizations, and others like them, are controlled by the Negro middle class and sponsored by white liberal monies. All these people treat history as if it were autonomous and had nothing to do with people or ideas. Old slavery, for instance, and its legacy, contemporary social and economic slavery, are looked at as hideous accidents for which no one should be blamed. (The liberal mind is such that it is already trying to persuade us that no one was to blame for Hitler, or for that matter, Joe Mc-Carthy, but "the times.") But the fact is that Negroes in America are still either field slaves or house slaves, the mode of oppression depending on the accident of social breeding, one group having easy chairs in its cells.

The puppet uses to which the historic Liberal/Missionary syndrome has put the black middle class have grown more bizarre through the years simply because of the increasing dead weight of the black poor which this artificial middle class is supposed to exorcise. But this weight, if anything, has gotten heavier, and is felt by all the elements of this society. The Welfare State was the reformer's answer. It was, and is, like a rotten blimp attached to the sleek new airliner. Thirty-five dollars a month and carfare to the Welfare office is available to each poor Negro who rides in this quasi-lighter-than-air ship called Ghetto. Each scream of agony that comes from the airship causes the black middle class, who ride in a special airtight compartment of the airliner, to ask for more Zweibacks in their gleaming bowls. So that now there must be a Negro Asst. Press Secretary, a proposed Negro Chief of Urban Affairs, a Negro for housing, etc., all of which creates a tiny transistor-like industry, for the placing of Negro tokens.

Booker Washington prepared the way for such utilization of Negroes. Martin Luther King, as a faceless social factor, is the same man. Both men are simply public servants. Washington solidified the separate but equal lie, when that lie was of value to the majority of intelligent white men. King's lie is that there is a moral requirement to be met before entrance into the secular kingdom of plenty. This is the reason Washington said

Negroes had to labor in the wings in the first place: to *get ready* for this entrance. Rev. King, who is formed very clearly and expertly from the same missionary fabric, comes bearing the same message of goodwill—that once this moral requirement is met by all Negroes (*i.e.*, the poor and brutalized will immediately rise once they understand this) then they might pass easily and joyously into that burning building which he insists on calling Heaven, even though gasoline is being spread on the blaze on all sides by every suffering man in the world. The reward for piety and high moral concern then is to be a membership in Gomorrah.

In this sense King's main function (as was Washington's) is to be an agent of the middle-class power structure, black and white. He has functioned in Montgomery, Albany, Birmingham, etc. (as has the Negro middle class in general) as a buffer, an informer, a cajoler against action not sanctioned by white Intelligence, however innocently these functions might collect as moral imperatives in his own mind. "Let it be our blood," he has said repeatedly to Negroes, and his sincerity on this point is not to be questioned. He is screaming out to the blimp with the loudspeaker of recent agonies. He is a hand-picked leader of the oppressed, but only the pickers are convinced.

For every token offered in the general interest of keeping goodwill between the black middle class and the Liberal/Missionary power structure, the gap between this invented bourgeoisie and the majority of black men in this country is widened. The tokens are more and more bizarre, have more and more supposed power and influence, but at each instance the poor black man gets even statistically poorer and less accessible to utopian propaganda. But the public servant function of the black middle class, especially as indicated by the performance of its chiefs like King, Roy Wilkins, Whitney Young, etc., is one of communication and control. That is, they present the "demands" of the black middle class to the white ruling class, and in exchange, as payment for the meeting of some of these demands—usually such social treachery as token integration which involves the creation of a lucrative civil rights *industry*—they relay that ruling class's wishes to the great mass of Negroes, while making sure that none of this mass becomes autonomous enough to make demands of its own.

The various vigilante middle-class groups like the first student sit-ins and the more militant chapters of CORE and SNCC began autonomously enough, but very soon they came into the fold of the mainstream moral suasion groups of which King is the titular if not actual head. The reduction of the Student Nonviolent Coordinating Committee to mere membership on the rolls of this main black middle-class reform element was signified quite blatantly by the censorship of its chairman's, John Lewis', speech at the March On Washington ceremonies. The Montgomery bus boycotts and later disorders, as well as the Birmingham near-violence before and after the bombings, were all quickly mounted by King, and brought to sanctimonious halts. Hours after the Birmingham bombings, King was already there, moving through crowds of Negroes, bringing them the word. Before that, when the Negroes were marching in that same city, King and the others, the leaders, swore that the white men were willing to bargain, if only the moral commitment could be made by black men. Absence of violence was the commitment these leaders asked, have always asked, and again it was given, by poor and lower middle-class Negroes and those strivers who had to be on the scene. And if word got back to the leaders that the silent weight, the poor blacks, were uneasy at being left to rot in the same ghettoes (without the slightest hope or chance of their misery being eased, except by making that symbolic leap into Bourgeois commitment, which is the local utopia) and dwelt by such uneasiness upon the impossibility of such advice, then King would walk among them praying, seeking to involve the most oppressed people in this country in a sham ethic that only has value for the middle-class power structure, and that even in those uses remains artificial, except as it maintains local and national social evils with an admirable stability. When this uneasiness would manifest itself as actuality or actual possibility, then these bearers of the missionary legacy would quickly seek to turn whatever energy that existed into confusion, and always shame. "Let it be our blood," King says to the poor, making an opportunistic identification he trusts even "backward" white people will understand as *leadership*. And when that cry of "passive resistance" is translated into common social activity, it means very simply, "Do as you have been doing, and some white miracle will prove your suffering was accidental, and finally worthwhile."

2

Violence or nonviolence as actualities have never been real categories. Rather, their use is symbolic in discussing possible goals of any Negro "progress" in this country (and the white West). Negroes, except for isolated, *i.e.*, limitedly organized and unconnected, incidents, have never been anything else but nonviolent. There have been race riots, when the "liberalizing" elements of the white power structure have been briefly stalemated, and the brainwashed lower-class and lower middle-class whites have clashed with those economically similar groups of Negroes. (In purely idealistic terms the real tragedy is that these two groups could not find goals that were mutually attainable in some kind of egalitarian "revolution" that would simply kill off their mutual oppressors and resurrect a "system" that would be workable for men who could utilize all their energies within it. Such a revolution was possible at the end of the Civil War. Marx did not study the racial situation in America closely enough, nor its macrocosm which has been worldwide since the white man realized, as E. Franklin Frazier says in his book *Race and Culture Contacts in the Modern World*, ". . . the extension of control over the colored peoples of the world." But the suspicions bred out of race ties, and in some cases inculcated in lower-class whites by upper-class whites purely for their own economic advantage, *e.g.*, at the end of the Civil War, are much stronger than any purely political method of organization.)

But for the most part there has been no violence from the black man. American Indians tried violently to defend their lands from white expansionism, but the material superiority of Western culture, and of the peculiar aggressiveness of humanist industrialism, was, of course, much too powerful. It is a humanist industrialism that has always longed for the twentieth century, *i.e.*, a century when man really is the measure, and literally has his fate clutched quite tightly in his spastic hands. A century where the only gods are immediately useful, and grow angry only as their worshipers do. The moral priggishness of the Western white man, which grows to insane proportions in America, is displayed religiously in every part of the world he has exploited. The ritual murders in the name of reason and progress go on every hour, in every part of the globe. How many nonwhite peoples have been killed in Asia, in Africa, in Latin America, just since 1945, in the name of some almost mystical need for a consistently accommodating order? The "Free World" is merely that part of the world in which the white man is free to do as he wants with the rest of the people there. And he has ruled this way since the Elizabethans.

When the white man says *violence*, he means first of all violence to his system, the possibility of outright war to change the political and economic categories of rule. But this has to do with thought, primarily, rather than the actual utilization of arms by Negroes to attain some arbitrary political and economic goals. The middle-class Negro's first word on the subject of violence, as it is sheepishly (and unintentionally) given reference as a possibility in the real world, is that, "We couldn't win anyway." But the real idea expressed here is that the bourgeois black man does not believe he could benefit by a total withdrawal from white society, which could be manifest by simple political rebellion. And in this sense any attempt at such rebellion represents "violence." (In the same sense, the political overtones of the Muslim movement represent this kind of violence against the lib-

eral middle-class missionary power structure, as withdrawal and actual political rebellion. This is why the
intelligent white man and the middle-class Negro are so
frightened of this group. Because, certainly, the only real
terror in Elijah Muhammad's program is the fact that
even though it utilizes a fancied ethnic hegemony as its
catalyst, its "goals" and its version of U.S. social history
are quite practical, as even a thinker like Thomas Jeffer-
son has attested. "The slave . . . when freed . . . is to be
removed beyond the reach of mixture . . .")

But a political rebellion within the existing social
structure is impossible. Any energy seen to exist within
the superstructure of American society is almost immediately harnessed within acceptable motifs, and shaped
for use by the mainstream, whether the results of this
process are called Swing music or CORE. The intent is
the same: *white music*. There is no way the black man can
be heard, or seen clearly, in the existing system. Muslims
would be rounded up and dropped in the Grand Canyon
before any kind of territorial gift would be made. Absolutely no "violence," no real social or political rebellion, will be tolerated by the static center, and for this
reason this center assumes a flexibility which allows it
to sweep from right to left without actually moving at
all. It merely gets stronger and essentially more intran-
sigent. "We will risk our cities to defend Berlin," is one
answer.

Since Negroes have never tried to mount any organized physical violence, and any political violence to the
system is, by the nature of the black man's oppression
almost impossible (even though there are attempts from
time to time, such as the new all black Freedom Now

party, which by the very exclusivity of its form proposes a very practical dissent, hence violence, to the existing party system), one might wonder just why it is so necessary for white liberals and the Negro middle class to exhort Negroes constantly to follow a path that, willingly or not, they have always followed? It would seem, if one examines the history of black men in the West, and especially in the United States, that they have most often been objects of violence rather than perpetrators. It would seem too that if there were any need to caution some group against violence, and influence them toward a path of righteous passivity and moral indignation, it would be the white man, at this point, who needed such persuasion. As exiled ex-NAACP leader Robert Williams has said, "How much money has been expended to convert the racist brutes of the social jungle of the South to the ism of nonviolence and love? How many nonviolent workshops are being conducted in Ku Klux Klan dominated communities and racist strongholds of hate and violence against Afro-Americans?"

Nonviolence, as a theory of social and political demeanor concerning American Negroes, means simply a continuation of the *status quo*. As this "theory" is applied to define specific terms of personal conduct Negroes are supposed to utilize, it assumes, again, the nature of that mysterious moral commitment Negro leaders say the black man must make to participate as a privileged class among the oppressed. Nonviolence on this personal (moral) level is the most sinister application of the Western method of confusing and subjugating peoples by convincing these peoples that the white West knows what is best for them. Since the Negro exists at a particular place in American society, which has been constantly redefined by the warring elements in white society, Nonviolence and Passive Resistance are only the echoes of a contemporary redefinition of the Negro's place, as seen by the most powerful of those elements, the industrial-liberal née missionary element, which since the Civil War has held the upper hand in the over-all power structure of the society. But even couched in purely secular terms, the emphasis on passive resistance and moral suasion is an undiluted leftover from the missionary era, and its intentions are exactly the same. Only God has been replaced, as he has all over the West, with respectability and air-conditioning. The Negro must have both before he is "ready" for equality is the way another answer goes. To enter into the mainstream of American society the Negro *must* lose all identity as a Negro, as a carrier of possible dissent. He must even assume a common cultural liability, and when the time comes for this white society to die, he will be asked to die with it, and for the same reasons it will die. But there is no indication that the poor have any such communal suicide in mind, not that they have any theories or bodies of social reasoning to the contrary; it is merely that in most parts of America the social system still hews to the intransigence of its beginnings and no real advance into that mainstream is really being offered. The white liberal's plan is still too academic to really work. But then what *will* happen? What will Negroes do? Are there any alternatives?

3

All black political thrusts, that is, any that could issue from the actual needs of the masses of Negroes, are blocked, either by the sham "leadership" of the middle-class Negro, whose whole tradition is based on selling out his poorer brothers, or by the intransigence of those whites who are "behind the times," as any liberal spokesman will tell them. An America made up strictly of such backward types of white men would survive only a few more years before internal disorder and/or external pressures resulted in out-and-out racial wars. (Asia, Africa, Latin America, and Black America versus the white West.) But the feigned flexibility of the center permits a certain toughness, for the American way that will take some pushing to topple completely. Nonviolence is such a feigned flexibility. It allows some gesture of social and political "protest," but offers no real alternative to the existing order. But, again, what is the black man's alternative? Very simply, either he must find some way to do political and social violence to the existing system, even though he is hampered at every step by the black middle class and the white power structure, or an actual physical violence will result.

When those four children were killed in the Birmingham bombing, the US Steel plant in that city should have been shut down by Negroes. Black workers should have walked out of every job they hold in the city. A general strike should have been called. An attempt should have been made to shut down completely the city's industrial resources. That city should have died, should have been killed by Negroes. At this writing the bombers have still not been found, and no attempts have been made toward finding an "equitable" position for Negroes in that city, if that's what was supposed to have happened. All of this happened two or three weeks after the great March On Washington. And nothing else could have shown the moral sham involved in that lugubrious display as horribly as that bombing. Martin Luther King arrived in Birmingham hours after the bombing to quiet the crowds and give a quiet light of hope to the middle class. But no real hope or stance is offered by black leaders in the face of such treachery. Talks in poolrooms with the "4th St. toughs," about the dignity of man, to men whose dignity consists in their constant resistance to the yoke of cultural compromise white men call their place. One young slick-haired cat chalking his cue and looking straight into the television camera, after that same bombing, said, "There's a whole lotta' people ain't gonna stand for much more 'a this." Meaning: "I am not the president's Assistant Press Secretary nor the first Negro to appear in a Chemical Corn Bank television commercial, but nobody's gonna run over me because of it."

The point is, I think, that the poor black realizes, at least instinctively, that no matter what deal goes down, *i.e.*, no matter which side "wins out," the "Crackers" or the Government, no help at all is being offered to him. The desegregation of schools has been largely a lie, the increase of employment among chronically unemployed Negroes has also not happened. The battle of housing is to determine whether a Negro who is able to buy a $12,000 house can live in it. There is no doubt that soon he might be able to, but that means little to most Negroes. At this moment even the administration's long touted civil rights bill is being systematically compromised by its supposed sponsors, not that it was very strong to begin with. A television commentator says it is a "reasonable" bill. Wish to God this man were black so he could get a good idea just how reasonable the bill is. Such a bill at its strongest is only a token, and has no practical application at all.

In the United Nations a few days ago only the United States, Great Britain, France, and the white "Free World" abstained from voting on a resolution to make illegal any organization that promotes race prejudice. In Latin America governments change hands monthly, and no matter how repressive, illegal, and non-representative a government might be, as long as it plays ball with the United States, is "anti-Communist," we say nothing. It is only in Cuba that something is going on of which we disapprove. But why? In South Vietnam and South Korea the United States supports the most brutal governments in the world. Part of the sugar quota is transferred to South Africa. We sign a new contract with Franco. And this is the society Rev. King wants to get the poor Negro ready to enter. Better Hell itself. But "partnership" in Gomorrah is the best thing offered by the white man to the Negro in America today. This is in essence what the promoters of Nonviolence represent to the Negro masses. The March On Washington, for instance, began as an idea of protest against the system, but was quickly turned into a nightclub act, and a "moral victory" for the middle classes, with marines and plainclothesmen on the scene just to make sure the audience liked the show they were going to put on.

Nonviolence then is not a protest at all, in the context it has been promoted into in America. It has to do with India too, just as Rev. King thinks it does. And just *what* did nonviolence accomplish there? The Germans were our enemies and they are better off than the great majority of Indians. Plague and hunger still ravage India: and for all the lies and rhetoric that issue from the West about that country's independence and the political individuality of Mr. Nehru, India for all practical purposes is still a crown colony. It is still very much exploited by Great Britain and the rest of the Western world.

Not only does Nonviolence usually mean no action at all, but it is not nor is it likely to be a useful moral concept in the impossible social environment of America, especially not the American South. One cannot draw analogies between American liberal proposals for Negro Nonviolence and the recent Algerian quietism under the terror of the OAS, simply because the Algerians were waiting for the French to clear out. It was a simple case of resisting a greater malice, knowing that the French troops would return if too many Colons were killed in retribution for the many Algerians who were killed during that period. It was a qualified military tactical device, which kept the French from marching back at the flank. But the Negro's "goal" has never, except in the late stages of slavery, been as clearly delineated as was the Algerians' in that situation. Nonviolence in the American context means, at its most honest evocation, a proposed immersion into the mainstream of a bankrupt American culture, and that's all. And as I have said, even the proposition is, finally, a fake. No such immersion is even possible. It is much too late.

A closer analogy is the fate of the European Jews, and more specifically the fate of German Jews at the hands of Adolph Hitler. The German Jews, at the time of Hitler's rise to power, were the most assimilated Jews in Europe. They believed, and with a great deal of emotional investment, that they were Germans. The middle-class German Jew, like the middle-class American Negro, had actually moved, in many instances, into the mainstream of the society, and wanted to believe as that mainstream did. Even when the anti-Jewish climate began to thicken and take on the heaviness of permanence, many middle-class Jews believed that it was only the poor Jews, who, perhaps rightly so, would suffer in such a climate.

Like these unfortunate Jews the middle-class Negro has no real program of rebellion against the *status quo* in America, quite frankly, because he believes he is pretty well off. The blatant cultural assassination, and the social and economic exploitation of most Negroes in this society, does not really impress him. The middle-class Negro's goal, like the rest of the American middle class, is to be ignorant comfortably.

What other goals can the Negro realize in America? The "out of date" white man, who is perhaps in one manner of speaking more honest, is offering the Negro nothing at all, except what has always been offered the black man in white society. He is saying if the Negro wants *anything* further than what the white man has always given he is going to have to take it. And this kind of white man will take steps immediately to see that such taking remains, as it has always remained, in the context of an "orderly" American society, unheard of. The liberal white man does not even offer the possibility of such "taking." His only goal for the Negro is that the Negro remain nonviolent. In exchange for this Nonviolence this liberal power structure will send an army into Mississippi to see that its symbols are accepted by white and black alike, but in essence this is all this power structure offers and what it hopes Negroes will continue to accept. It offers Negroes nothing further in their or its life time. Nonviolence, then, is not being offered as a means to an end, but as the end in itself.

The Negro's real problem remains in finding some actual goal to work toward. A complete equality of means is impossible in the present state of American society. And even if it were possible, the society is horrible enough without Negroes swelling its ranks. The only genuine way, it seems to me, for the Negro to achieve a personal autonomy, this equality of means, would be as a truly active moralizing force within or *against* American society as it now stands. In this sense I advocate a violence, a literal murdering of the American socio-political stance, not only as it directly concerns American Negroes, but in terms of its stranglehold on most of the modern world.

The Negro must take an extreme stance, must attack the white man's system, using his own chains to help beat that system into submission and actual change. The black man is the only revolutionary force in American society today, if only by default. The supposed Christian ideal of Nonviolence is aimed at quieting even this most natural of insurrectionary elements. As an actual moral category all rational men are essentially nonviolent, except in defense of their lives. To ask that the black man not even defend himself (as Robert Williams tried to defend himself and the rest of the black community of Monroe, North Carolina, a few years ago, before he was framed in a bogus kidnapping charge by local whites with the aid of the Federal Government) is to ask that

that black man stay quiet in his chains while the most "liberal" elements in this country saw away at those chains with make-believe saws. The Negro, again, in this instance, is asked to be what the white man makes of him. Not only does the white man oppress the Negro, but he is even going to tell him how to react under the oppression. Surely, however, the most patiently Christian man must realize that self-defense in any situation is honest and natural. It is also obligatory, otherwise there is no use in asking for any right since the asker will probably not be around to benefit by its granting.

But if the most violent political and social protests are muffled (and the exile of Robert Williams seems to me one notable example of such muffling; the attempted jailing of newsman William Worthy for trying to find out about China and Cuba another) and the moral bankruptcy of the black middle class continues to be used by the white ruling class as its cynical symbol of Negro "progress," then it seems to me that quite soon an actual physical violence *will* break out. For every lie that the liberal power structure tells itself, the black bourgeoisie, and the rest of the world about the majority of Negroes in this country, alienates that majority even more critically. By not allowing a real "grassroots" protest to issue from the core of the oppressed black masses, the American white man is forcing another kind of protest to take shape. One that will shake this whole society at its foundations, and succeed in changing it, if only into something worse.

Soon, for every sham gesture like the March On Washington or the still impending "deal" King and the other black "leaders" made with white Birmingham, there may be twice that many acts of unorganized responsive violence. How much longer does anyone in this country, black or white, think that the "4th St. toughs," *i.e.*, the oppressed black man, who has made no deals with the white power structure, nor received any favors, is going to run from policeman and dogs, or stand by and watch while "unknown assailants" blow up their pitiful homes? Is it possible that the American white man knows so little about Negroes, from whatever level he does his observing, that he thinks these Negroes believe or have ever believed in the justice and morality of the white man? Left to their own devices, the masses of Negroes will finally strike back, perhaps even kill, in a vertiginous gesture of fear and despair. Their anger will not even matter, since it has been a hopelessly familiar element in their emotional lives.

Nonviolence can be your "goal" if you are already sitting in a comfortable house being brought the news of your oppression over television. It *can* be the normal conduct of rational men if they can believe in the literalness and effectiveness of what they are trying to accomplish by such conduct. But walk, on any night, from one end of 125th Street (in New York's Harlem) to the other, and count the hundred policemen and figure out the climate of rational conduct that is being cultivated by such an environment.

A legitimate Negro protest movement unstalemated by the sham of tokenism and filthy bourgeois intention might succeed in remaking this society, and establishing an honest connection between it and the rest of the nonwhite world. But most of the leaders of what passes as such protest, the middle-class Negroes and white liberals, who have access to courtrooms and picket lines, have already sold their souls. Finally, it would seem that for the mass of Negroes such leadership as they need will be spawned within their own ranks, bolstered by those young Negroes from the middle class who recognize themselves the hopelessness of their social connections. But this leadership is most likely to take solid form only in the most repressive and irrational of circumstances. The most horrible vision I have is that the white man, in growing terror of those suddenly ubiquitous acts of unorganized violence to which the most oppressed black men might resort, will become even more repressive, and even the veneer of the liberal establishment will be stripped away (in much the same way that such veneer has been worn away in international affairs or in dealing with the possibility of actual domestic political dissent. The Communist party is already outlawed. Mail is being opened. Phones are being tapped. The penalty for traveling to Cuba is five years in prison and five thousand dollars fine, they say. Where will such insanity lead?). And in such instances these unconnected acts of responsive violence would increase, and perhaps even gradually find their connection. The result of such chaos is anybody's guess. Guerilla warfare, concentration camps? But one of our congressmen has said recently that our only real ally in Africa is South Africa. And the only "foolproof" way to completely stop legitimate Negro protest, especially as it grows more agitated by the lies and malice of most of America, and agitated, I am saying, into actual bloodletting, would be to follow the South African example (or Hitler's). I hope this is ugly fantasy too. But there are very few white men in this country who are doing anything to prevent this. The present emphasis on Nonviolence rather than honest attempts at socio-economic reconstruction will only speed the coming of such horror.

the dempsey-liston fight*

S ee?
See him dream?

See the white man dream? Which is where the whole race has gone: to the slowest. But the mass media make this dream a communal fulfillment, so that now, each man who had and has the dream in solitary can share, and grow bigger at its concrete illustration.

Sonny Liston is the big black Negro in every white man's hallway, waiting to do him in, deal him under for all the hurts white men, through their arbitrary order, have been able to inflict on the world. But since the American black man has been closest to, and in *that* sense been most debased by the source and fortune of this philosophical malady, the black man is the local symbol of an entire world of hatred. Sonny Liston is "the huge Negro," the "bad nigger," a heavy-faced replica of every whipped up woogie in the world. He is the underdeveloped, have-not (politically naïve), backward country, the subject people, finally here to collect his pound of flesh.

The mock contest between Liston and Patterson was a "brushfire" limited war (as Neo-Colonial policy) to confuse the issue. Optimistic diplomacy to obscure the balance of power. Patterson was to represent the

* Inspired by an article, "The Greatest Fights Of The Century," in *Esquire* magazine, December 1963.

fruit of the missionary ethic, in its use as a policy of the democratic liberal imperialist state. Patterson had found God, had reversed his under-privileged (uncontrolled) violence and turned it to work, and for this act become an object of prestige within the existing system. The tardy black Horatio Alger, the glad hand of integration, to welcome those 20,000,000 chimerically, into the lunatic asylum of white America.

In this context, Liston, the unreformed, Liston the vulgar, Liston the violent (who still had to make some gesture toward the Christian ethic, like the quick trip to the Denver priest, to see if somehow the chief whitie could turn him into a regular fella) comes on as the straightup Heavy. I mean "they" painted Liston Black. They painted Patterson White. And that was the simple conflict. Which way would the black man go?

The last question traveled on all levels through the society, if anyone remembers. Pollsters wanted the colored man in the street's opinion. "Sir, who do you *hope* comes out on top in this fight?" A lot of Negroes said Patterson. (That old hope come back on you, that somehow this *is* my country, and ought'n I be allowed to live in it, I mean, to make it. From the bottom to the top? Only the poorest black men have never fallen, at least temporarily, for the success story.) A lot of Negroes said Liston.

A white cab driver was turning to see me in his rear view mirror; he said, "You know that Liston has got the biggest hands of any boxer to come in the ring. You know his arms are six feet long. I mean six feet long each. He's like an animal. Jesus! He shouldn't even be allowed to fight normal guys. He's like an animal." And that's the word from that vector from polite society. Strictly, an animal.

And it meant a lot to the Liberal/Missionary syndrome that they test their handiwork against this frightening brute. So a thin-willed lower middle-class American was led to beatings just short of actual slaughter, to prove the fallibility of another artifact of American culture (which, like most of its other artifacts, suffers very seriously from built-in obsolescence). This happened twice. And each time Patterson fell, there was a vision that came to me of the whole colonial West crumbling in some sinister silence, like the across-the-tracks House of Usher.

But, dig it, there is no white man in the world who wants to fight Sonny Liston himself. (Though Cassius Clay has come from the Special Products Division of Madison Avenue to see what he can do.*)

Now the Orwell Synapse takes over. (What we cannot gain from experience, we will gain by *inperience*.) That is, as every totalitarian order has done, history is changed to correspond with what we all know reality *should* be. It's like the European painters when they began to paint Arab/Moorish/Semitic experience in medieval middle-European contexts. (Christ is then a blond who looks like Jeffrey Hunter. Another smart Germanic type made good.) For this reason, in order to find out what really is the simple history of this country, for example, one has to go to E. Franklin Frazier and W.E.B. DuBois. *Inperience* is the positing of a fantasy "event" as what is the case. Practically speaking, for instance, if God were not white, how could he get permission from the white

* See Dempsey-Liston Addenda.

man to make him? If, say, God were black, there would have to be some white man somewhere to tell him what to do, right?

In the magazine, Liston beats Marciano, "the most brutal first round ever seen," and he also beats Louis, ". . . Louis flew back five feet, fell, and rolled on his face." And having set this up, Dempsey comes marching in like drunk Ward Bond whistling a cavalry tune, to straighten everything out. It was a little hectic (like in *The Spoilers*, or where John Wayne is facing a really brave Indian) but the end, I am certain, is never in doubt. Even in dirty books there has to be some moral reestablishment. As the barbarian climbs through that chink in the wall, IBM!, ". . . Liston turned and fell heavily to the floor, his right glove under his face." In the posture of sleep, like a gypsy in the desert, a *fellaheen*. "At six, he rolled over and, back now in his corner, Dempsey smiled." The muscular Neyland-Smith.

So now, forget that all this is dream and wish fulfillment, and think of it as it does now, and must necessarily, sit—as a blatant social gesture. This is how the synapse works. We erase the mad-bad big black bad guy by going back in time to get him in a dream, and the drop to the canvas takes nearly the whole of the dream, it is so slow and gravity-less, or maybe it is replayed, reseen, over and over again. ". . . heavily to the floor, his right glove under his face." We get the big strong likable immigrant, who has always done America's chores. He's glad to oblige. We always get to the bad niggers . . . either kill 'em, or drive 'em out of the country. Jack Johnson, Henry Higland Garnet, DuBois, Paul Robeson, Robert Williams, Richard Wright, Sidney Bechet, Josephine Baker,

Beauford Delaney, Chester Himes, so many others. All the black neurotic beauties trailing dumbly through the "equal" streets of hopeless European cities. All the unclaimed fugitive corpses.

But this was the calmest and most rational method. Simply going back like in a science fiction story called *By His Bootstraps*, and erasing this loud black fool. Add to the record book, just before the Tunney fight, "Liston vs Dempsey. . . . . . . .Dempsey, K.O., 1:44 of the ninth." (And in the doing, of course, Louis is turned off as well.)

What kind of men are these who would practice such deception on themselves? (The will and promise of the entire society has grown just as weak, perhaps now even more so since it has lost the strong man who at least offered the fiction of its vitality.) Oh, they are simply Americans, and some years from now, perhaps there will be this short addition: "You remember them, don't you?"

Dempsey-Liston Addenda

This image, observation, was made pre-Liston-Clay, also before Mohammad Ali or Cassius X emerged. Now I think of Clay as merely a terribly stretched out young man with problems one would have hoped would have at least waited for him to reach full manhood. Clay is not a fake, and even his blustering and playground poetry are valid, and demonstrate, as far as I'm concerned, that a new and more complicated generation has moved onto the scene. And in this last sense Clay is definitely my man. However, his choosing Elijah Muhammad over Malcolm X, if indeed such is the case, means that he is still a "homeboy," embracing this folksy vector straight out of the hard spiritualism of poor Negro aspiration, *i.e.*, he is right now just angry rather than intellectually (socio-politically) motivated.

The Liston-Clay fight seemed to be on the up and up to me. Liston was just way out of shape, expecting young X to be just another weak-faced American. But Cassius can box, and Liston in shape might have trouble spearing the very quick X. But poor Sonny's in jail now,* where most of the white world would have him. (Shades of Jack Johnson!) And the possibility of a return between Clay and Liston grows each day more remote.

But whoever has the heavyweight championship now, or in the future, it is an even remoter possibility that it will be Jack Dempsey, or for that matter any of his Irish progeny. Most of the Dempseys in America now don't have to knock heads for a living (except as honest patrolmen) and their new roles as just anybody, having mostly graduated from the immigrant-newcomer class, make them as weak and unfit for the task of defeating any of the black heavyweights as any other white Americans, even the honorary kind like Floyd Patterson.

* 1963.

black writing

The black man in Writing is the same as the anyplace (USA) Negro. Except that black writers, like any writers, can be more specific about the nature of their own connection with whatever America they happen to wake up in. So, if a writer knows some things about Negroes In General (a small town in Calissippi) or for that matter, if he knows some things about almost any Negro, here, then he can at least make generalizations about a great many Negroes that might be valid. That is, about their connection with America.

The first thing any writer wants to do is write, I'd suppose. (Though this is not at all true, finally, when you look up and find yourself straddling some lady, or foot up on a bar rail. But ideally the writing would be the thing, for writers.) Any writer can write. Black writers can write. To publish is what most writers want next. Publishers are usually not very intelligent, or they might be intelligent, but it's usually hard to tell. Publishers don't publish a lot of fine books they should publish. Some of these fine books are written by black writers.

Negro Material, is what publishers (who, as I have said, are not very intelligent) call stuff written by Negroes about themselves. Negro Material is *hot* right now, to quote a knowledgeable white man. But even hot, there are many books by Negroes that will not be published because they, the publishers will tell you, "duplicate our other Negro material." Though, of course, they will publish as many duplicated junks about ofays as they can. The commercial novel, in America, is just that—a duplication of tired white lives. But listen, you Negroes, this *is* the white man's country (the way it's run), and the image of America, as it has been separated from truth or actuality (*e.g.*, by the cool words of the white rich into the ear of the white poor), is a white one. In one sense we are fortunate, because when a black man sees some incredibly inane bullshit on TV, for instance, he can feel happy that it is Charlie that that machine presents, and represents, and not ever the black man. And really there's no reason for a lot of Negro Material, like they say, to interest the publishing industry as a whole, because publishers are interested in market just like any other industrialists. A book—no matter what you have to say in it—is just a commercial object, and Negro Material is not the commercial object that gets the best sales. But even so, there are always exceptions. Baldwin books sell. Ellison, and some others. And actually there are a great many Negro writers somehow in print, very regularly—thinking from the small magazines to books. You can be Frank Yerby, speaking from the vantage point of raceless historical sex fantasy, and make all the loot you want—but then you have to be an American. (Though Yerby is cooler than that and has moved out, he is still one of the money-lenders—but his books are always good for at least one hard-on, as I remember.) But at the level where writing counts (for something besides money), *i.e.*, from head to page, nobody gets in the way—not even Charles. And this *is* important.

I've had experience now with people not liking this and that because it's this way and that way, when finally what they meant was to deny that I had real access to a real world, that is, to deny that what I was presenting was fact—not filth, or pornography, or obscenity. You are supposed to present, and represent, the middle-class (middlebrow) ofay world, and if you do not do that—no matter what color you are—you're in trouble, as far as publishing is concerned. The Negro writer writing about his own life is in trouble too—so that some maniac can say to you, as Gregory Corso said to me recently, "Black writers are stuck because they're always talking about their people." There is no real answer to that. But who does anyone talk about? Hemingway is always talking about his people, or Joyce. What does anyone think The Dubliners were—abstract literary categories? It is simply, again, that someone is trying to tell you write is white.

But a man is supposed to write about what he knows and feels, can understand about the world and his life in it. If I fill a book up with 8,000,000 white people, it is still Negro material; a Negro put them there, colored them (white) with the pigment of his experience. And whether or not I label each page "written by coon," the fact of the thing is that each page, and the experience, etc. on the page, was collected by that coon too. And, finally, it is my world, too. Get to that.

The most serious problem facing Negro writers, it has seemed to me, and again it is pretty much the same problem that faces any Negro, is that for so long now the white man has told him that his, the Negro's, version of America and the world is shameful fantasy. That such an America, or world, does not really exist. But then this same kind of lie has been told to white people too, especially to those white people who also had a version of America that did not agree with the merchant's reality. So that for instance books by white writers like William Burroughs or Edward Dorn or John Rechy or Hubert Selby show an America as alien to the fattest inhabitants of this society as any honest black man's emotional history.

I think though that there are now a great many young black writers in America who do realize that their customary isolation from the mainstream is a valuable way into any description they might make of an America. In fact, it is just this alienation that could serve to make a very powerful American literature, since its hypothetical writers function in many senses within the main structure of the American society as well. The Negro, as he exists in America now, and has always existed in this place (certainly after formal slavery), is a natural nonconformist. Being black in a society where such a state is an extreme liability is the most extreme form of nonconformity available. The point is, of course, that this nonconformity should be put to use. The vantage point is classically perfect—outside and inside at the same time. Think of the great Irish writers—Wilde, Yeats, Shaw, Synge, Joyce, O'Casey, Beckett, etc.—and their clear and powerful understanding (social, as well as aesthetic) of where they were and how best they could function inside and outside the imaginary English society, even going so far as teaching the mainstreamers their own language, and revitalizing it in the doing.

Let no one convince any black man that he is an

American like anybody else. The black writer should be deaf to such misinformation, especially since he can *prove* (*vide*: Chester Himes' books, DuBois' *Black Reconstruction* or Wright's *Black Boy* and *Native Son*, Franklin Frazier's works, especially *Black Bourgeoisie* and *Race and Culture Contacts in the Modern World*, Baldwin's *Native Son* and *Go Tell It . . .* as staggering for instances) that something quite different is the case. And these proofs should be published by black men themselves, if no other way is available. There is no reason any intelligent man should have it easy in America—especially not any intelligent black man. We know that.

expressive language

Speech is the effective form of a culture. Any shape or cluster of human history still apparent in the conscious and unconscious habit of groups of people is what I mean by culture. All culture is necessarily profound. The very fact of its longevity, of its being what it is, *culture*, the epic memory of practical tradition, means that it is profound. But the inherent profundity of culture does not necessarily mean that its *uses* (and they are as various as the human condition) will be profound. German culture is profound. Generically. Its uses, however, are specific, as are all uses . . . of ideas, inventions, products of nature. And specificity, as a right and passion of human life, breeds what it breeds as a result of its context.

Context, in this instance, is most dramatically social. And the social, though it must be rooted, as are all evidences of existence, in culture, depends for its impetus for the most part on a multiplicity of influences. Other cultures, for instance. Perhaps, and this is a common occurrence, the reaction or interreaction of one culture on another can produce a social context that will extend or influence any culture in many strange directions.

Social also means *economic*, as any reader of nineteenth-century European philosophy will understand. The economic is part of the social—and in our time much more so than what we have known as the spiritual or meta-physical, because the most valuable canons of power have either been reduced or traduced into stricter economic terms. That is, there has been a shift in the actual meaning of the world since Dante lived. As if Brooks Adams were right. Money does not mean the same thing to me it must mean to a rich man. I cannot, right now, think of one meaning to name. This is not so simple to understand. Even as a simple term of the English language, *money* does not possess the same meanings for the rich man as it does for me, a lower-middle-class American, albeit of laughably "aristocratic" pretensions. What possibly can "money" mean to a poor man? And I am not talking now about those courageous products of our permissive society who walk knowledgeably into "poverty" as they would into a public toilet. I mean, The Poor.

I look in my pocket; I have seventy cents. Possibly I can buy a beer. A quart of ale, specifically. Then I will have twenty cents with which to annoy and seduce my fingers when they wearily search for gainful employment. I have no idea at this moment what that seventy cents will mean to my neighbor around the corner, a poor Puerto Rican man I have seen hopefully watching my plastic garbage can. But I am certain it cannot mean the same thing. Say to David Rockefeller, "I have money," and he will think you mean something entirely different. That is, if you also dress the part. He would not for a moment think, "Seventy cents." But then neither would many New York painters.

Speech, the way one describes the natural proposition of being alive, is much more crucial than even most artists realize. Semantic philosophers are certainly correct in their emphasis on the final dictation of words over their users. But they often neglect to point out that, after all, it is the actual importance, *power*, of the words that remains so finally crucial. Words have users, but as well, users have words. And it is the users that establish the world's realities. Realities being those fantasies that control your immediate span of life. Usually they are not your own fantasies, *i.e.*, they belong to governments, traditions, etc., which, it must be clear by now, can make for conflict with the singular human life all ways. The fantasy of America might hurt you, but it is what should be meant when one talks of "reality." Not only the things you can touch or see, but the things that make such touching or seeing "normal." Then words, like their users, have a hegemony. Socially—which is final, right now. If you are some kind of artist, you naturally might think this is not so. There is the future. But *immortality* is a kind of drug, I think—one that leads to happiness at the thought of death. Myself, I would rather live forever . . . just to make sure.

The social hegemony, one's position in society, enforces more specifically one's terms (even the vulgar have "pull"). Even to the mode of speech. But also it makes these terms an available explanation of any social hierarchy, so that the words themselves become, even informally, laws. And of course they are usually very quickly stitched together to make formal statutes only fools or the faithfully intrepid would dare to question beyond immediate necessity.

The culture of the powerful is very infectious for the sophisticated, and strongly addictive. To be any kind of "success" one must be fluent in this culture. Know the words of the users, the semantic rituals of power. This is a way into wherever it is you are not now, but wish, very desperately, to get into.

Even speech then signals a fluency in this culture. A knowledge at least. "He's an educated man," is the barest acknowledgment of such fluency . . . in any time. "He's hip," my friends might say. They connote a similar entrance.

And it is certainly the meanings of words that are most important, even if they are no longer consciously acknowledged, but merely, by their use, trip a familiar lever of social accord. To recreate instantly the understood hierarchy of social, and by doing that, cultural, importance. And cultures are thought by most people in the world to do their business merely by being hierarchies. Certainly this is true in the West, in as simple a manifestation as Xenophobia, the naïve bridegroom of anti-human feeling, or in economic terms, Colonialism. For instance, when the first Africans were brought into the New World, it was thought that it was all right for them to be slaves because "they were heathens." It is a perfectly logical assumption.

And it follows, of course, that slavery would have been an even stranger phenomenon had the Africans spoken English when they first got here. It would have complicated things. Very soon after the first generations of Afro-Americans mastered this language, they invented white people called Abolitionists.

Words' meanings, but also the rhythm and syntax that frame and propel their concatenation, seek their culture as the final reference for what they are describing of the world. An A flat played twice on the same saxophone by two different men does not have to sound the same. If these men have different ideas of what they want this note to do, the note will not sound the same. Culture is the form, the overall structure of organized thought (as well as emotion and spiritual pretension). There are many cultures. Many ways of organizing thought, or having thought organized. That is, the form of thought's passage through the world will take on as many diverse shapes as there are diverse groups of travelers. Environment is one organizer of *groups*, at any level of its meaning. People who live in Newark, New Jersey, are organized, for whatever purpose, as Newarkers. It begins that simply. Another manifestation, at a slightly more complex level, can be the fact that blues singers from the Midwest sing through their noses. There is an explanation past the geographical, but that's the idea in tabloid. And singing through the nose does propose that the definition of singing be altered . . . even if ever so slightly. (At this point where someone's definitions must be changed, we are flitting around at the outskirts of the old city of Aesthetics. A solemn ghost town. Though some of the bones of reason can still be gathered there.)

But we still need definitions, even if there already are many. The dullest men are always satisfied that a dictionary lists everything in the world. They don't care that you may find out something *extra*, which one day might even be valuable to them. Of course, by that time it might even be in the dictionary, or at least they'd hope so, if you asked them directly.

But for every item in the world, there are a multiplicity of definitions that fit. And every word we use *could* mean something else. And at the same time. The culture fixes the use, and usage. And in "pluralistic" America, one should always listen very closely when he is being talked to. The speaker might mean something completely different from what we think we're hearing. "Where is your pot?"

I heard an old Negro street singer last week, Reverend Pearly Brown, singing, "God don't never change!" This is a precise thing he is singing. He does not mean "God does not ever change!" He means "God don't never change!" The difference, and I said it was crucial, is in the final human reference . . . the form of passage through the world. A man who is rich and famous who sings, "God don't never change," is confirming his hegemony and good fortune . . . or merely calling the bank. A blind hopeless black American is saying something very different. He is telling you about the extraordinary order of the world. But he is not telling you about his "fate." Fate is a luxury available only to those fortunate citizens with alternatives. The view from the top of the hill is not the same as that from the bottom of the hill. Nor are most viewers at either end of the hill, even certain that, in fact, there is any other place from which to look. Looking down usually eliminates the possibility of understanding what it must be like to look up. Or try to imagine yourself as not existing. It is difficult, but poets and politicians try every other day.

Being told to "speak proper," meaning that you become fluent with the jargon of power, is also a part of not "speaking proper." That is, the culture which desperately understands that it does not "speak proper," or is not fluent with the terms of social strength, also understands somewhere that its desire to gain such fluency is done at a terrifying risk. The bourgeois Negro accepts such risk as profit. But does *close-ter* (in the context of "jes a close-ter, walk withee") mean the same thing as *closer*? Close-ter, in the term of its user is, believe me, exact. It means a quality of existence, of actual physical disposition perhaps . . . in its manifestation as a *tone* and *rhythm* by which people live, most often in response to common modes of thought best enforced by some factor of environmental emotion that is exact and specific. Even the picture it summons is different, and certainly the "Thee" that is used to connect the implied "Me" with, is different. The God of the damned cannot know the God of the damner, that is, cannot know he is God. As no Blues person can really believe emotionally in Pascal's God, or Wittgenstein's question, "Can the concept of God exist in a perfectly logical language?" Answer: "God don't never change."

Communication is only important because it is the broadest root of education. And all cultures communicate exactly what they have, a powerful motley of experience.

1964

hunting is not those heads on the wall

Thought is more important than art. Without thought, art could certainly not exist. Art is one of many products of thought. An impressive one, perhaps the most impressive one, but to revere art, and have no understanding of the process that forces it into existence, is finally not even to understand what art is.

The artist is cursed with his artifact, which exists without and despite him. And even though the process, in good art, is everywhere perceptible, the risk of perfection corrupts the lazy public into accepting the material *in place of* what it is only the remains of.

The academic Western mind is the best example of the substitution of artifact worship for the lightning awareness of the art process. Even the artist is more valuable than his artifact, because the art process goes on in his mind. But the process itself is the most important quality because it can transform and create, and its only form is possibility. The artifact, because it assumes one form, is only that particular quality or idea. It is, in this sense, after the fact, and is only important because it remarks on its source.

The academician, the aesthete, are like deists whose specific corruption of mysticism is to worship things, thinking that they are God (thought, the process) too. But art is not capable of thought. Just as things are not capable of God, but the reverse is what we mean by the God function, the process I am talking about.

The Supermaker, is what the Greeks identified as "Gods." But here the emphasis is still muddled, since it is what the God can do that is really important, not the fact that he is the God. I speak of the *verb process*, the doing, the coming into being, the at-the-time-of. Which is why we think there is particular value in live music, contemplating the artifact as it arrives, listening to it emerge. *There* it is. And *There*.

But even this is after the fact. Music, the most valuable of artifacts, because it is the most abstract, is still not the activity that makes itself possible. Music is what is left after what? *That* is important.

A museum is a curious graveyard of thinking. But we can go through one hoping to get some inkling of what those various creators who made the creations were thinking. What was he thinking when he did That? is a common question. The answer is obvious, though: That.

Formal art, that is, artifacts made to cohere to pre-conceived forms, is almost devoid of this verb value. Usually a man playing Bach is only demonstrating his music lessons; the contemporary sonneteer, his ability to organize intellectual materials. But nothing that already exists is *that* valuable. The most valuable quality in life is the will to existence, the unconnected zoom, which finally becomes in anyone's hands whatever part of it he could collect. Like dipping cups of water from the falls. Which is what the artist does. Fools want to dictate what kind of dipper he uses.

Art is like speech, for instance, in that it is at the end, and a shadowy replica, of another operation, thought. And even to name something, is to wait for it in the place you think it will pass. Thought, "I've written"—understanding even this process is recording. Art-ing is what makes art, and is thereby more valuable. But we speak of the Muse, to make even the verb a thing.

If we describe a man by his life we are making him a verb, which is the only valid method since everything else is too arbitrary. The clearest description of now is the present participle, which if the activity described continues is always correct. Walking is not past or future. Be-ing, the most complex, since it goes on as itself, as adjective-verb, and at the moment of. Art is not a be-ing, but a Being, the simple noun. It is not the verb, but its product. Worship the verb, if you need something. Then even God is after the fact, since He is the leavings of God-ing. The verb-God, is where it is, the container of all possibility. Art, like time, is the measurement of. Make no mistake.

Even "sense" is clearly a use some energy is put to. No one should fool around with art who is only trying to "make sense." We are all full of meaning and content, but to make that wild grab for more! To make words surprise themselves. Some more of the zoom trembling in its cage, where some fool will be impressed by its "perfection." This is what should be meant by a "primitive" mind, that which is satisfied with simple order. But "using" words denies the full possibility of expression, which is, we must suppose, impossible, since it could not be stopped and identified. Art is identification, and the slowing-down for it. But hunting is *not* those heads on the wall.

The imitator is the most pitiful phenomenon since he is like a man who eats garbage. A saxophonist who continues to "play like" Charlie Parker cannot understand that Charlie Parker wasn't certain that what had happened had to sound like that. But if a man tries to understand *why* Parker sounded like he did, the real value of his music begins to be understood.

Form is simply *how* a thing exists (or what a thing exists as). When we speak of man, we ask, "How does he make it?" Content is *why* a thing exists. Every thing has both these qualities; otherwise it could not (does not) exist. The art object has a special relationship between these two qualities, but they are not separable in any object.

The recent concern in the West for the found object and chance composition is an attempt to get closer to the non-Western concept of natural expression as an Art object, since of course such an object has form and content in special relationship like any thing a man made. Because a man cannot make a thing that is in this sense unnatural. The unnatural aspect of the man-made object is that it seems to exist only as a result of man, with no other real connection with the nonhuman world. *Artificial*, in this sense, is simply *made*. "Bad art" is usually unnatural, *i.e.*, it seems as if it could not exist without being made by a man. It is strictly artificial.

Western men have always been more concerned with the artifact, the made thing, as "an art" separated from some natural use. Art as a separate category of concern is first seen when? Functional art is as old as man was when he made *anything*. To posit the idea that you will make a thing whose sole value and function is that you will make it, is a different emphasis.

God (which is separate, and before, A God) is in one sense an art object and was probably the first. In the secular West, God is a nonfunctional (literally) art object. But earlier, God was simply the naming of force, in the same sense I meant earlier of naming a thing by its life. God was "the force out of which the world (and life) issued." The *naming*, nominalization, of that force is finally a step at making it artificial. The arbitrary assignment of content (which means nothing in a strictly local context, *i.e.*, Who will object?) based very likely on need, is the beginning of God as an art object.

But think about this, "the force out of which the world (and life) issued" exists everywhere, as we can see, and this is the basic form (and content) of God. Everything else is most likely to be nationalism. Nothing else exists. But again the confusing of process with artifact, or rather the substitution of process for artifact. When God gets to be a thing, it is an artifact. When the lightning was "the force out of which the world issued," the emphasis was on natural evidence, the natural thing. And lightning is curiously apt, since in its natural form, it is a process, a happening, as well as an artifact. Duplicating God signs was simple education.

When God started to *look like* a human being, men had gotten very sure of themselves. (That is, once the dog, the wolf, the fish, the bear, the leopard, etc., had all been God, and the fallacy of this reasoning, in whatever turn of environmental circumstance, became traditional. Some of the things we have seen are animals, possibly one of them is God. Men next.) But *naming* is the first appropriation, the earliest humanist trend. Jane Harrison says the Greeks took the fear away by not only making all the various qualities known in the world men, but understandable, knowable, men. They began to make lives for their Gods, so those Gods could only exist in that certain way. From the unknown verb, to the familiar artifact. Greek Gods are beautiful Greeks, which finally in social/political terms is the beginning of modern nationalism. What the Western white man calls the beginning of democracy was the positing of the sovereign state, wherein everyone was free. The rest of the world could be exploited. *Logos*, then, is not merely thought, but belief. Greeks were Greeks because they had the same beliefs. A Greek was a man who believed the Gods were Greeks.

Humanism is good in this sense, that it puts the emphasis on what we actually have, but there is a *loss* with the loss of the unspecific imagination because knowing man was all there was enabled the less imaginative to show up fully armed. Man's mind is revered and, in the ugliest emphasis, man's inventions. Again the hideous artifact, to replace the valuable process. The most stupid man ought to know he is more important than what he can make. But he will never understand that what moves him is even more important, because of the con-

temporary (post-Renaissance) loss of prestige for the un-
seen. When God had a rep, his curious "workings" were
given deference. But now that everything is grounded or
lodged in the sweaty palm, men only believe in what, as
Auden inferred, "takes up space."

Thinking, in the most exalted humanist terms, is
God, the force out of which the world issued. Nature,
we make a "natural" process. Darwinian determinism
provided the frame. From the Renaissance, the boost of
the industrial revolution, and man surrounded by his
artifacts. Machines, which are completely knowable.

leroi jones talking

"Jones seems to have been taken in, to believe that white society actually reflects the nature of white men."
—Michael Smith, *Village Voice*

Prologue

I write now, full of trepidation, because I know the death this society intends for me. I see Jimmy Baldwin almost unable to write about himself anymore. I've seen DuBois, Wright, Chester Himes, driven away—Ellison silenced and fidgeting in some college. I think I almost feel the same forces massing against me, almost before I've begun. But let them understand that this is a fight without quarter, and I am very fast.

This is a society which has little use for anything except gain. All is hacked down in its service, whether people, ideas, or ideals. The writer, say, who achieves some entrance into the mainstream of American letters is almost immediately in jeopardy of being stripped of his insight by the ruffians of "success." A man who writes plays and poems, for instance, is asked to be a civil rights reporter, or write a dopey musical—if he is talked about widely enough—if not, there is no mention of him, and perhaps he is left to rot in some pitiful mistake of a college out in Idaho. A man who writes or makes beautiful music will be asked to immortalize a soap, or make sounds behind the hero while that blond worthy seduces the virgins of our nation's guilt. Even a man who is a great center fielder will still be asked to kick up his heels at Las Vegas. My God, where are we? What is this place? What is the reason—and in this most prosperous of all utopias—for the existence, everywhere in it, of filth, ignorance, cowardice? You name it.

For those of you who do not know my name, I am what is called "A Negro Writer." I write what is commonly called "Negro Literature." What these terms usually mean (I mean somewhere below the veil of anxious politeness smart Americans think of as their image) is that the people who can be tagged with them produce a variety of writing that should be thought of as second rate, in much the same way all American literature was thought of before Melville, Poe, James, etc. But the reasons for this low estimate of black writing have not, I think, been fully understood. And I mean the estimate made by the official estimators, the deciders of what is of intellectual, hence emotional, value in the society, *i.e.*, what can be carried off and deposited in that huge junk heap of useless artifacts called Culture.

As some way into an analysis of these estimators, and they are the soul of the American Academy, I can begin by saying these are the same people, the same minds, who would teach unsuspecting high school children that American Literature is Longfellow or *The Yearling*, when we have had great poets like Whitman and Dickinson. And what is the basis for their estimates? What pushes them grimly and consistently toward ideas and intellectual penchants that are only sanctified by mediocrity? I would say probably their lives, and the intellectual gracelessness to which those lives are anchored. The last refuge of the basest puritan/colonial temperament—a temperament that in purely social terms could send Ethan Allen to the hills or Robert Williams into exile in Cuba.

This temperament, which when canonized and strengthened becomes an academy, or institution, or establishment—though I am speaking now specifically of arts and letters—is identical with the temperament that controls (but not necessarily animates) this society at all levels. It is a temperament whose champions can speak ecstatically of progress yet allow such a thing as Harlem to exist and spell out the lie of their intentions. (And make no mistake, Harlem, as only a quick example, only exists because the establishment this temperament animates needs it to exist. If it did not want that place, and the nightmare of its implication, to exist, Harlem would be removed by the time this article appears.) The people who are committed to waging war around the globe to maintain the glories of unnatural advantage are brothers of the people, say, who thought that *How to Succeed in Business* . . . deserved the Pulitzer Prize. And ironically, they are right, finally, since that prize has long been removed from the concern of people interested in telling about the world as it really is rather than flattering those shabby pilgrims whose word, in this life at least, is law. People the poet Charles Olson spoke of as "the pimps of progress." But they are not simply "people," they are, sadly, a nation. I will make my case clearer.

A Negro writer, if he is to get at that place in his being (a verb/participle) where art lives, must do as any other artist, *i.e.*, find out what part of that be-ing is most valuable, and then transfer that energy (again paraphrasing Olson) from where he got it on over to any reader. And by reader I mean simply the openness of infinite "interpretation" as it can be said to reside in an artifact, if that artifact—a play, a solo, a poem, a form of loving—be faithfully made. An artist, any artist, must say where it is in the world that he actually is. And by doing this he will also say who he is. But no matter what a man tries, the products of his thinking, indeed of his life, will identify who and where, and for most Americans this is unfortunate, since they are weakling murderers and liars and the place where they live is named after them, even if the plastic sign on their desks says poet and another on the door says CopOut U.

But what of the man, black or white, going as artist, who does not have such signs to confuse reality, who remains simple minded in that he believes that everything is valuable that men have experienced, because posed against that experience—and it is available as light is, or air—there is only darkness, or, not even that. What of that man? And I aspire to be such when I am not drugged or drunk. What can such a man hope to *prove* by continuing to live in this hip flophouse of the universe? I suppose only that even here some actual reality—not lies, or flattery, or soap selling—some real feeling perhaps, can continue to exist even in the most adverse conditions, as, say, Dante saw Beatrice even in Hell.

For one thing, the denial of reality has been institutionalized in America, which is what I was talking about before. And any honest man, especially an artist, must suffer for it. But that is the most blatant method of that

institution's perpetuation: the suffering of the honest, or
the naïve. The artist is both. For he is a man who would
say not only that the king has no clothes, but proceed
from there to note how badly the sovereign is hung.
Such a man is, of course, crazy—just as I am, something
like Kit Smart or Blake or Rimbaud or Allen Ginsberg.
We're all ravers, in one fashion or another. Something
else I aspire to is the craziness of all honest men. (And
as another aside: one way Negroes could force this institutionalized dishonesty to crumble and its apolo-
gizers to break and run even faster than they are now
would be to turn crazy, to bring out a little American
dada, Ornette Coleman style, and chase these perverts
into the ocean, where they belong. Say, if Negroes just
stopped behaving, stopped being what Charles desires,
and just flip, go raving in the streets, screaming in verse
an honest history of America, walk off their jobs—as
they should have done in Birmingham after those children were murdered—and watch the country grind to
a halt, the owners cracking their knuckles as they got
out their gold guns and got ready to blow out their own
legendary brains. It is a good, and practical, idea. Why
don't you try it, Negroes?) That is, a craziness that will
make a man keep talking even after everyone else says
he shouldn't.

In America—I haven't lived anywhere else as long—
the art that is most admired is an art that will tell the
basest elements of the society—and I do not mean the
poor, Mr. Luce—that they are still gods, or at least interesting. And I do not even mean the George Wallaces
or Ross Barnetts, who are, after all, only stooges for the
mighty, since they have to take abuse. The mighty never

take abuse. I mean the Du Ponts, United Fruit, General Motors, Remington, Standard Oil, IBM, and the rest: the owners. You name them. All the officials of this society, the influencers, the make-out artists, their stooges—the fashionable "disengaged" dispersers of lies—all the talented compromising swine who will smile in your face, knowing your life is in their hands. If our armies want to invade some place why don't they invade the vaults of Alcoa and publish their horrible records? Yet it is not merely Big Business that is responsible for the hopelessness of this society, but all the people in this nation who somehow benefit by their owners' conduct. All the people who somehow have something to lose. Only one question I have to ask such people, "That thing you have to lose . . . where did you get it? Is it yours?"

And, of course, the easiest people to single out for such questioning are our dizzy middle class. They are the ones who benefit, as much as they can and with a knowledge of the methods employed, from the murderous intentions of our "leaders." But whatever I say, they are already damned by their lives. Turn on a television, what do you see? Who is responsible for it? They are the people who have something to lose, and are already damned by their lives.

But there are people in America not responsible for the filth of its image. (What is that image? Ask any Latin American.) Most Negroes, for instance, are not responsible for, nor are they represented by, the consistent insipidity and vapidness, and again, the denials of reality, flashed at us constantly through the mass media of the society. Those messages are from the owners' minds— Negroes are not owners . . . no, not even those flashy tokens of the missionary mentality, one of whom might even be lucky enough to be The First Negro To Push The Button For An Atomic Murder, as *Ebony* magazine might say—they are just liberals' gibberish. So that now most Negroes can say of that mass media, "That's Whitie doing that stupid thing . . . not me," and be right, essentially. But even so, Negroes had better dig themselves, and find out what they really want. Some men like being slaves. Others would rather die.

And apart from social investigation, any honest man in America is separate, or separates himself, from the gloss of its image. But by being separate from that image a man is also setting himself up to be murdered, one way or another. Specifically, the writer in America, if he is to be canonized along with the mediocre and the misunderstood, must reflect the mores, needs, etc., of that institutionalized temperament sloppily called The Establishment. That is, a poem must be not only understandable, but gratifying, to that Establishment, which as I said before is gratified only by gain and the falsification of reality required to transform its essential filth into some delightful euphemism even Presidents can quote without fear of saying something meaningful. A poem or play, to use my own personal insistence, should also even beatify that Establishment, perhaps in a pastoral recollection of the joys of luxurious ignorance, *e.g.*, "This Connecticut landscape would have pleased Vermeer," as one poet, Kenneth Koch, has satirized such glorious banality. But the poet or playwright (artist) who would actually say something about the actual world of living and dying, and not merely reflect in some flattering miasma of fake meticulousness only that portion of creation understood and enjoyed by the new masses (a middle class that knows no hard and fast economic delineation, only that intellectual and emotional aura which can be translated into all the pettiness and vulgarity these citizens hold in common), is in trouble. Very few people in this society are interested in such a place as the real world. Because were they really interested in reality, not as sociology or style but as intellectual and emotional fact, then the suicidal core of this society would swell and explode, and, hopefully, perhaps even the owners might be faced with the fact of their evil just before they did themselves in.

But to get back specifically to Negro Writing, the Negro writer is in a peculiar position because if he is honest, most of what he has seen and experienced in America will not flatter it nor can that seeing and experiencing be translated honestly into art by euphemism. And while this is true of any good writer in America, black or white, it is a little weirder for the Negro, since if that Negro is writing about his own life and his own experience, that writing must be separated from what the owners and the estimators think of as reality, not only by the intellectual gulf that causes any serious man to be estranged from the mainstream of American life, but by the social and cultural estrangement from that mainstream that has characterized Negro life in America which his work will reflect.

The mainstream mentality does not even know what a Negro is. That is why it keeps asking, "What does the Negro want?" What does any man *want*? To be left alone with his life, and have some hope of making that life what he wants it to be. And Negroes, when they make art, must carry the weight of white America's social and cultural stupidity, as well as the ordinary burden of art's responsibilities. So that, for instance, when any Negro shows up in a play, the mainstream mentality can only see that Negro as an advertisement for the NAACP, but very rarely as a man. But Negroes are men, and their minds and emotions have human shapes which cannot be categorized, even admirably, by the missionaries, their opposites. To white America the Negro is a shadowy abstraction reflecting the sterility of its own needs. They can think of Negroes only with abstract nonhuman concepts. So that, for example, some critic can say of the character Clay in *Dutchman*, that he is ". . . not Negro enough," meaning, of course, that this critic has a definition of what a Negro, any Negro, is. Or, this same critic can say, of Clay's death, that he does not die the death of a Negro, but of a naif. But can't a Negro be a naif? And what is "the death of a Negro"? Has that been institutionalized too?

Another recurring criticism of the play *Dutchman* was that the white girl, Lula, was too crazy, too neurotic, too extreme, etc. Critics wanted also to know, in what I think ought to be an obvious paranoid plea for "understanding," was this girl supposed to be all white people. But how can one white person be all white persons, unless all white persons are alike. Are they? Similarly, it is equally stupid to think of the Negro boy as all Negroes, even though, as I've said, most white people do think of black men simply as Negroes, and not as individual men. But I showed one white girl and one Negro boy in that play, and the play is about one white girl and one Negro boy, just them, singularly, in what I hope was a revelation of private and shared anguish, which because I dealt with it specifically would somehow convey an emotional force from where I got it—the discovery of America—on over to any viewer. But for the feeble-minded, black and white are always the most important aspects of anything, not what a thing really is, but how it can be made to seem, if it is to accommodate the silly vision of the world they are stuck with.

But I will say this, if the girl (or the boy) in that play has to "represent" anything, I mean if she must be symbolic in the way demented academicians use the term, she does not exist at all. She is not meant to be a symbol—nor is Clay—but a real person, a real thing, in a real world. She does not represent any thing—she is one. And perhaps that thing is America, or at least its spirit. You remember America, don't you, where they have unsolved murders happening before your eyes on television. How crazy, extreme, neurotic, does that sound? Lula, for all her alleged insanity, just barely reflects the insanity of this hideous place. And Clay is a young boy trying desperately to become a man. *Dutchman* is about the difficulty of becoming a man in America. It is very difficult, to be sure, if you are black, but I think it is now much harder to become one if you're white. In fact, you will find very few white American males with the slightest knowledge of what manhood involves. They are too busy running the world, or running from it.

the last days of the american empire
(including some instructions for black people)

NEWS PICTURES

i nformation
Death throes of the empire. UGLY CRACKERS! Negro policemen with sad twisted eyes. Strong faces (big Mammas with their arms folded, lonely children whose future lives you wonder about), black faces set into America. There is no America without those whites of eyes against black skin . . .

ALL KINDS OF VICTIMS. People being burned.

What does America mean to you? Does it mean what these pictures say? Well it do. It sure do. It surely definitely absolutely does. This is world America. You are in the trance of the White People. You will be escorted to your cell. In fact you will be pre-born into your cell. "And there you can be quaint in our lighter moments. Now, for christ sakes, you have to admit that Mantan Moreland was funny." (This man I was talking to meant "amusing.")

Is there anyone in the real world America who thinks Slavery Has Been Abolished? Or for that matter, another irrelevance, would there be someone in the statesies so stoned, as would qualify America as being less sick than the invention of Lee Oswald? (Many oil men are inventors, and they have weird hobbies, like their freakish fakeman brothers, bombing churchchildren through the tobacco spit of their brains.)

These pictures should make anybody think. This is what America looks like now. Where is the hope? Why should this terrible place not fall? Who can *dare* defend it? Look at your LEADERS. What do they look like? Do they look like you, any of you??? If they do, then you have something to lose. And chances are you'll lose it.

It is the blackness of the sufferers, their absolute existence as a *different race*, that cheapens any further social description as to what, actually, is going on? Explanation is a selfish act. But The Man says, What's going on? What do you mean people are suffering? I didn't realize . . . What? That it was real and really happening and real and really happening, but only to the niggers, and those white people too stupid to be rich in this last fat bastion of the white man, doomed now to go down hard, and eaten, smashed at, from its insides by its acquisitions, and the "holiness" of them. Black People will prove to be the most costly of those acquisitions.

The white eyes of those who say (and with them the brutal cuteness of the Negro middle class, who perhaps will never understand what's really going on till they reexamine the value of their social connections, *i.e.*, it is a scientific guess that the white man will not be El Hombre too much longer, *i.e.*, you cannot fail to recognize the difference between Boone, Daniel and Boone, Pat), How can these people live this way? Why don't they do something? No one ought to deny the validity of that question. Finally our enemies are right. Why don't they do something?

Maybe what a few of the white eyes saw, showing up

in Bedford Stuyvesant, or St. Francesville, Louisiana—to catch a part of time-now, to be exposed to a reality, a basic truth of the world—filthy makeshift playgrounds, the children's eyes deep in their black skin, woodplank streets in parts of black Brooklyn, and summer, everybody outside, children playing on their knees, men sitting or walking slowly, or staring, or laid out in the street dying in sneakers—these are truths the television will not even use as news, except when the people out on those streets start moving, like they did "last summer," and being thrashed for at least assuming the dignity of an organism that will react when it is struck. This is the rest of the world. This is what the good white man cannot connect himself with; cannot or will not, it makes no real difference, the results are the same. Most white men I meet say they are not responsible. Perhaps it is best to be left there. To take them at their word, that I'm hip, you are not responsible to the world. But you will be held responsible, anyway, since you own it, you think.

But then, who demands these whippings and bombings? Is J. Edgar Hoover an intelligent man? Will Lyndon B. Johnson submit to an aptitude test? Why isn't automation a help to man? Who is H. L. Hunt? Is there any reason why all the world should be working and dying and growing hopeless with rage, just to feed fat white faces? What is this bullshit?

Black people, if you can steal this expensive book, at your liberal employer's, for instance, though he may even be "a friend of your people"—just remember the only reason you are there in the first place is *for the money, to stay alive, to survive*—steal this book, it will make you very very hot, but even so you will learn that your brothers and sisters are strong, strong, under all the horrors of The White Hell. And in seeing the horrors, and by becoming angry, but even beyond that anger realizing what strength you have—YOU BLACK PEOPLE ARE STRONG, remember that—then you will realize that it is now not even the time to be angry, I mean so angry that you will not remember that you are strong, much stronger than the white eyes. Then you will not need to be angry any longer, you will have gotten to that point, where you will be absolutely rational. Our singing is beautiful, but we can sing while we move. MOVE!

To be rational now in this insane asylum, where we are held prisoner by the inmates. They want us to be their keepers. Do you Negroes like being keepers for these sadists? But to be rational. Rational men would do something to stop the mad, before they destroy not only the asylum, but the rest of the world. There is no reason why we should allow the white man to destroy the world, just because he will not share it, will not share it with the *majority*. The nerve, the stupid arrogance, the ignorance, AND FEAR, in those cracker eyes, those firemen, state patrolmen, the dog holders, all that fear is in the bones of this society. Those mad white policemen are the soul of this society. And their technology has made them strong. We have accepted that technology, as fact, as useful to our dreams, etc., but its owners are mad, because they do not value reality, and therefore they are not real. Hollow Men, Paper Tigers, Closet Queens of the Universe.

Look at those weak fag faces on those patrolmen arresting that beautiful chick, and finally there is something in her face which is stronger than anything in white eyes' life. Because she has had to live in a world of extremes, which is the widening of the consciousness. And this is the "hip" syndrome, simple awareness—America will make you aware if you are black. So that, for instance, in any argument with a liberal white man, finally the black man must grow speechless with rage, because there is always a point beyond which no black-white argument can be pushed with reason. We know what has happened to us, to our mothers and fathers. What more can be said? The black man was brought to the West in chains, he is still in chains. He is still a captive, Negroes, a captive people. What can you say? Look at any pictures of America. They must show the final impasse between white America and Black America. Pictures like these should be used when the black man runs out of words. When the exasperation of explaining his life to justify his desires makes him silent with rage, in the face of *any* white man.

There is an absolute gulf that separates white from black. Slave/Slave Master are two different worlds. Segregation reinforces itself, spawns, continues, *separate* cultures. So the Beatles can make millions of dollars putting on a sophisticated coon show, which drives weak white girls into gism fits—all that energy and force, but even so transmuted and disguised. But it is still the Chuck Berrys, the Muddy Waters', etc., who first harnessed that energy. The Ornette Colemans. No matter the use such changed and weakened force might be put to in Winosha, Wisconsin, or by Lynda-Bird's fake Watusi, the real power remains where it naturally falls.

The force of the Negro's life in America has always

been very evident in America, no matter the lengths to which white Americans have tried to hide and obfuscate it. But I mean you cannot, for instance, blame any white man for liking Andre Previn more than Cecil Taylor; it is his life that is reflected by his choices (is, in fact, those choices). Most white men in America are closer to Andre Previn than CT or Duke Ellington either, for that matter. White America reflects its energies by its choices. You think that the heroimage in American flicks is homosexual merely by *chance*?

Reality is only useful to people who have some use for it. Otherwise they get something else. But everybody's got to pay some kind of dues, one way or another. It won't even matter, finally, if the person happens to be "innocent"; there is no such thing. If you are alive, now, you are involved with now, even if only by default. You know what "Germans" still means. First of all, now, it means liar. No matter what the man can tell you, *e.g.*, "I was head of the anti Nazi forces, etc., etc.," the word "German" is sufficient to give any story the shakes. What? you will say. What . . . are you talking about . . . aren't you a German? And that's the end of that. In a few years, "American" will have that connotation, for the rest of the world. (In most of the world it has that connotation already.) And, even more horrible, it will not even matter to the rest of the world that the Negro was "the victim," etc. People will simply ask, Why? And, given the plausibility of supposing that most men would rather not be victims, the fact will remain that any "answer" to that Why? will have to be shaky. The only answer could be, I was in the trance of the white people. But that is a cop out, I'm afraid. Your questioner will not even bother to point out certain obvious alternatives. You will be listed simply as "Coward."

But there are many Negroes now, young and otherwise, who have no use for the role (of victim) the white man has cast him in. Again, look at the black faces. The young boys marching across the street with their signs, or the young fox wet and screaming her defiance, her hatred, but most of all her *will* to live, and to fight back. Look at the young Northern middle-class black lady sitting demurely on the pavement surrounded by cops. Look at her face and posture. You cannot lie to this woman. She knows you're lying. She reads the *Times*. She knows the *New York Times* lies. The poor black man will not even have had to read it to know it lies. "It's whitey's paper, ain't it? What you expect?" Right again. (I looked at a photograph of a black cop arresting a black woman.) Dig for a few seconds, the big spook cop's mouth. He's got his lips pinched together, staring at the lady. BLACK NEW YORK COP SGT. NUMBER 67, YOU KNOW YOU'RE WRONG!! YOU ARE FIGHTING YOUR OWN PEOPLE!

Another sense gotten from any true picture of this society is the isolation of the black man in America. He is a different race from the white man. The poor white has been brainwashed into wanting to kill the black man, so that black man won't get his job or his little girl's drawers. All the immigrants to this country, the Italians, the Irish, the Jews, etc., where are they in this struggle? All the white people in America who have grounds for dissent, and will not dissent. They have had to pay a price for their shaky seat in this enterprise. The dues I spoke of, which even they have had to pay, is to be mistreated, used, duped, and still put out on the street to handle America's light work. Where are the Italian Anarchists? The Sacco-Vanzetti frame put them on the skids, and the Mafia takes up the wild strong ones whose lifeneeds still put them outside straightup WASP-AMERICA. The Jewish Radicals, Socialists, Communists, etc., of the 30's, what happened to them? Have they all disappeared into those sullen suburbs hoping Norman Podhoretz or Leslie Fiedler will say something real? The price the immigrants paid to get into America was that they had to become Americans. The black man *cannot* become an American (unless we get a different set of *rules*) because he is black. And even the hopeless CORE representative I met who claimed black men were as evil as white men can never become a white man. Though he might desire it more than anything in the universe. He cannot change the one thing about him that is most important in this place. He must remain, even deluded, a certain kind of black man. The black man's dissent cannot be gotten rid of. It just builds. And builds.

But the white man splits the black man into cadres, "classes," when there is none except blackness—which the white man is the first to realize. Against the filth of America (and with it, the white West—the British, the French, the Germans, the Belgians, the Portuguese, the Dutch, etc., and their ugly little roles in Asia, Africa, Latin America) the black man has to be absolutely *together* in order to survive. But too often, certainly most times in the past, the white man has been able to win out, maintain his stranglehold on us, merely because most of us were so busy looking out for ourselves, which is the "ME ONLY" syndrome, that we were willing to let the worst things in the world happen to our brothers. With black people all over the world dying the most horrible kinds of death imaginable some fools would still be walking around with their behinds in the air saying, "But I'm Cool." Well the word is No You're Not, not as long as one of your brothers and sisters is being messed over by "the man."

Get it together! We must lock arms, take each other's hand, and never stop working until the stone is rolled over this deep stinking hole even some of our "civil rights leaders" speak of as if it were paradise.

Since this book is so expensive, it will fall into the hands of more MC Negroes than people out on the block. (MC meaning middle class or master of ceremonies, and in America the ceremony is blood violence and hatred.)

MC Negroes, I know you can still be made angry too. Perhaps something in the faces of white terrorists will frighten you out from under your shaky cover stories; cover stories like "middle class" or "college trained" or "qualified Negro" or any other fake entrances into this crumbling Rome, which somehow cut off your testicles, usually with the hard cold edge of a dollar bill. ANYBODY CAN PRINT MONEY! BUT NOT EVERYBODY CAN LIVE IN THE WORLD WITH THE PEACEFUL STRENGTH OF THE TRULY VIRTUOUS MAN. (White Americans cannot.)

If you have made some "progress," or somehow got your hands on a good taste of white eyes' loot, keep it moving among your people; also your knowledge. We are in this *together*, let us help each other and begin rolling that huge black stone. *Most* of the world is with us.

I cannot repeat it too many times, nor can any of you

black people repeat it too many times to one another. DO NOT ALLOW YOURSELF TO BE SEPARATED from your brothers and sisters, or your culture. This is what makes us think we are weak. But we are not weak. Remember the stories of your parents and grandparents. We have survived over three hundred years of the worst treatment possible, and still come up strong. All Charles has to show for those years is his loot, but the world changes each second, and Charles' hands grow more and more spastic, his lies more and more obvious. For instance, where would the US Olympic Team be without the black man??? This analogy can be extended into any meaningful level of American life. The black man should dig, for instance, that he is one of the chief reasons this society, these Mad American White People (. . . MAWPS . . .) can continue to exercise their will over the rest of the world. We black people, by our labor, are supporting these murderers. It is a paradox, but one no black man should fail to recognize. Even the isolated Negro who has gained "acceptance" into this Gomorrah, or the hard-working black man in a "defense" plant or steel mill, must realize the vicious uses his entrance into the mainstream will be put to. All you Negroes making "good livings" now, do you know what the fruits of your labor are being used for? Usually your labors contribute heavily to the murders of nonwhite peoples all over the globe.

Where have all these "police actions" in which the U.S. has taken the major part since the Second World War been happening? And police action is a good phrase because that's what white eye is now—anywhere—a policeman working feverishly to keep the nonwhite peoples down, in colonial or semi-slave positions whether they are American Negroes, Africans, Asians, or Latin Americans. It's all the same. The same mad white people you see in any *Life Magazine* home are our real "ambassadors" all over the world; spiritual cops and cretins. (Do you think that the television series *Burke's Law*, where the hero is a white millionaire who is also chief of police, is *accidental*? This is the way these folks think, and what they legitimately aspire to. Ditto, in the case of James Bond, the suave, unbeatable fascist. All these things merely prepare the American's psyche for his role in world domination.)

What I am saying is that there is *no chance* that the American white man will change. Why should he? Isn't this the richest nation in the world? The gross national product rose to $624 billion this year, the growth figure over last year's $584 billion is about $45 billion. This money is not being made because the white eye is ready to "understand" the needs of the world, but because he has been even more successful recently in suppressing those needs. Can there be even one American so out of it as not to realize that this money, this luxury, exists only at the expense of the rest of the world's peoples? Can there be a Negro so out of it as not to understand that the worst racists in South Africa are brothers to the men he sees in our newspapers daily being celebrated for their "humanity"? It is sickening, for instance, to see in our free newspapers accounts every day of how the white man is trying to save the world. This is true. He is trying to save the world—as his personal victory garden and commode. As for instance, in the Congo, where thousands of black people are slaughtered to make the world safe for the white man. The only difference between the Congo and, say, Philadelphia, Mississippi, is the method the white man employs to suppress and murder; essentially, it is the same scene, the same people dying for the same reasons. And of course, they are the same murderers who kill our people all over the globe.

But it sickens me to know that there are supposedly intelligent black people walking around who would actually believe that the Belgians and Americans flew those paratroopers into the Congo for humanitarian reasons. My God! You mean Charles would send planeloads of paratroopers (plus those divisions of white mercenaries) into the Congo to save . . . how many? twenty-one white hostages? and yet still be unable to send even one Vietnamese helicopter to Mississippi to find out who assassinated Medgar Evers, or maybe one Special Forces (anti-liberation "guerillas") to Birmingham, so maybe just one shred of information might be turned up concerning the identities of the dynamite murderers of those four little church children.

Does it make sense to any of you that Uncle Sap will spend millions to "put West Germany back on its feet," and yet have a place such as Harlem in the world's showplace, which they will not spend one honest nickel to alter or intelligently repair? And there are Harlems in every American city where there are great numbers of Negroes. But even more diabolical is this fact, that even the most liberal white man in America does not want to see the existing system really *changed*. What this liberal white man wants is for the black man somehow to be "elevated" Martin Luther King style so that he might be able to enter this society with some kind of general prosperity and join the white man in a truly democratic defense of this cancer, which would make the black man equally culpable for the evil done to the rest of the world. The liberal white man wants the black man to learn to love this America as much as he does, so that the black man will want to murder the world's peoples, his own brothers and sisters, Moise Tshombe style. And let no black man forget all the black traitors all over the world, most of whom, like Tshombe or JaJa Wachuku of Nigeria, have been so brainwashed that they might even think what they are doing (*i.e.*, helping in the murder of thousands of black people) is right. One man, an American Negro, George Schuyler, has even come out on the side of a straightup oppressor, Portugal, defending its actions in Angola where it murdered thousands of black Africans. Black people, do not forget Negroes like this, remember them and every detail of their treason. It will help us to be more scientific.

But these are the Last Days Of The American Empire. Understand that Lyndon Johnson is a war criminal of the not so distant future. Understand that the power structure that controls this country and the world has grown desperate . . . in the face of so much prosperity, but prosperity that is coupled with more unrest than ever before. There are wars of national liberation going on all over the world. The Second World War made emphatic America's newly won security as absolute world ruler, but it also shook up most of the other colonial empires of the world. The need to have that war seen as "A War Against Fascism" contributed dramatically to the organization of many of the world's colonial peoples into armed nationalistic liberation fronts who saw as their task, even after the war against fascism, the eradication of any form of colonialism or imperialism. British, French, and Dutch colonialism suffered almost irreparable losses, but these sorry people are still trying, by one ruse or another, to regain control of their subject peoples. But where before there were only cries of outrage now these European white eyes are met with bullets and bombs.

There is a war of liberation going on now in America, although the black American has still not gotten hip enough to organize a National Liberation Front that would include all groups and aspirations, and sweep, by the increase of its power, right over this failing power structure, and push these sadists and perverts into the sea. That is the unity that is needed. When will we be strong enough and wise enough to commit ourselves to this kind of unity?

In one sense, when I speak of unity, I mean that seeing one young man being followed menacingly down a road by half the Crackers in Georgia, makes me wonder what it was, specifically, that moved him to do this. I want to know what was he thinking, sprawled in the dust, holding his head, knees pulled up against his chest? I want to know did this young black man really feel that by letting some subhuman superfools abuse and beat him, he was somehow accomplishing something? That is, I cannot yet understand what kind of mind shift I would have to undergo, for instance, so that I would be convinced, as these rednecks were working me over, that I was doing something to break Charlie's back. The unity I desire would be most apparent when most Black People realized that the murderous philosophies of the

Western white man take many curious forms. And that one of the most bizarre methods the man has yet to utilize against black people is to instruct large masses of black people that they are to control their tempers, turn the other cheek, etc., in the presence of, but even more so under the feet and will of, the most brutal killers the world has yet produced.

The kind of unity I would want to see among black Americans would at least produce a huge WHY? when some gentle oppressor talked convincingly about pacifism and nonviolence. In the white West nonviolence means simply doing nothing to change this pitiful society, just do as you have been doing, e.g., suffer, and by some beautiful future-type miracle the minds of the masses of white men will be changed, and they will finally come around to understanding that the majority of peoples in the world deserve to live in that world, no longer plagued by the white man's disgusting habits. But why, WHY, must anyone wait until these cretins . . . change . . . ha ha . . . their famous minds, before people are permitted to live with the simple dignity any man ought to know? Why indeed? The answer is that these askers for nonviolence, i.e., virtuous stagnation, are usually people who would suffer, or at least think they would, if this society were changed with the suddenness of the next second. Even the black man who preaches nonviolence is essentially functioning under the trance of the white people. There are black men who love the white man so dearly, who love, I must suppose, the nice warm feeling of shoe sole on their woolly heads, that they would do nothing to see that the white man relinquishes his stranglehold on the world. But then, there are other black people in America and the rest of the world who will not rest until that stranglehold is broken. So poised against the image of the young man hugging his knees in the dust, there are also images of young men and old men silhouetted on their porches with their rifles, watchful all through long black Southern nights, men who have no desire to be masters or slaves, but who cannot live in the world as it is without at least attempting to defend what little of the world they know is theirs. I look at an old man sitting next to his gun, or a young man holding his like in a photo to be sent back to a girlfriend, and I wonder about the young man holding his head in the dust. I wonder also about Robert Williams, the ex-NAACP leader from Monroe, North Carolina, who was framed on a kidnapping charge by local officials with the help of the Federal Government simply because he had "advocated" that black men realize that they were living among savages and barbarians and that they must protect themselves and their families, because the Government was made up of these same savages and barbarians. Mr. Williams is in exile in Cuba now for that reason; that he made a few rational statements about the nature of the white American, and what possibly ought to be done when faced with one, and such reasoning is dangerous to the white man, and the white man will have none of it.

The kind of unity I would like to see among black Americans is a unity that would permit most of them to understand that the murder of Patrice Lumumba in the Congo and the murder of Medgar Evers were conducted by the same people. I want them also to realize that a man like Robert Williams faced the same fate, for the same reasons. I want them to realize that any attempt the black man makes to be seen or heard, clearly, honestly, from where he has been made to live during the three-hundred-odd year residency in the West, is always met with repression and violence. Or else such attempts will be subverted by the wills of the holiest of white men, the liberals, who do not want to be our bosses, but our guides. But listen, black men, these liberals are usually agents. That is, even though what these men say might seems to come freely out of an untroubled heart, chances are these words, *e.g.,* "moderation," pacifism, nonviolence, gradualism, etc., etc., seek merely to dim your passion and turn your most rational needs and desires into evil fantasies white (and black) schoolchildren condemn when they are learning to count. Ask the next white liberal you meet, would he be willing to let you, you black man, be his, this white man's, "spiritual guide." And also when the next white man comes up to you and describes the sparkling democratic utopias of the future, remember that he is asking you to pull your knees up against your chest, head hidden, and dream in the dust of never-never land. And when the next missionary comes on to you about nonviolence use his own bible as your lever, pointing out that the God of the Jews was not particularly interested in turning cheeks, *viz.,* all those drowned Egyptians.

But opposed to that image of dreaming in the dust, there is the image of one brother with the sign reading NOW. Look at his face—there's nothing any kind of missionary type could tell this man. He looks like he's beyond all the loads of buckrogers happiness bullshit, and is demanding simple truth. And the sign says NOW, which is clear enough. In news photos all over America there are many other signs of the times: LOVE THY NEIGHBOR (a sign maybe which ought to sit in huge letters in the White House and Pentagon and CIA); WHO NEEDS NIGGERS (from the self-confessed purest of whities); WHERE IS DEMOCRACY (a woman with a very good question); FREEDOM (the most ambiguous term known to man, if Barry Goldwater, the "half-Jewish" Übermensch, can use it, to rally his 25,000,000, and Martin Luther King can use it, presumably with a different sense intended. But to BG freedom means, like they say, free enterprise, which means OPEN YOUR POCKETS 80 per cent of the world, big white meatface wants to get his rocks off!! That is the freedom to murder, rob, and lie to any people who stand in the way of your own holy luxury.). There is also a sign, on an old beatup Southern store, that reads NEGRO KEEP OUT. There are signs like this all over America. And where there are no written signs, brains have been marked, so that the same sentiment leaps out of people's eyes. And finally, the paradox is that these people are right: NEGRO STAY OUT! Because now, when Charles is up tight all over the world, and will of course ask the black lackeys to help him out, it is high time the black man began to make use of the Tonto-syndrome, *i.e.*, leave The Lone Ranger to his own devices, and his own kind of death.

There are pictures of very old black men and women in the news too. Some of the faces look as if they were too old to be lied to. And there is an essential unity existing among these old faces that can no longer be put on by trinkets and fake wampum, and the face of the young man with the NOW sign, just above his eyes. Add to these images, the images of the black men standing on their porches with their rifles looking into a night made unfriendly by the hideousness of the white man's ego, and you will probably get a sense of the powerful emotions and will for release that is crackling in the psyches of the majority of black men today. But there are crucial American social paradoxes that the black man must also understand if he is really to understand the nature of his enemy. For instance, Negroes have been killed and beaten in Mississippi, Alabama, etc., for even attempting to register to vote. In the North, Negroes have long mustered a heavy voting bloc, and because of this have some degree of token political power. But the ugly paradox is to be seen everywhere in the North, the promised land. This token political power can do nothing to change the basic structure of the society. This society, for as long as it has functioned, was never meant to be equitable as far as black men were concerned. It was made for the white man, and the black man was brought here only to be *used*, to promote the luxury of the white man. That was the only reason. It still is the only reason the black man is alive in the West today, that continued exploitative use. But one day, and very soon, the white man might just look up, hip again, and see that the black man has outlived his usefulness. Then the murders will break out in earnest.

So it is a very grim spectacle to see all these Negroes beaten and brutalized for trying to vote, and some ofays must fall on the floor laughing every time they think of it. Because finally in those Southern states, or in the rest of America for that matter, who could you vote for, Negro? I mean, do you really think that by your getting a chance to vote on these criminals who run for political office in America, that somehow you'll be getting closer to peace and social justice? You cannot really think that! I cannot believe that you can still believe that, after so many years of lies and abuse. The choice on almost any level you care to name is roughly like that contest between Lyndon Johnson and Barry Goldwater, in the South most times even worse—and if there's any black man anywhere in the world who thinks that either one of those chumps is working for him, he is laboring under a hideous delusion, or else maybe he is in the Tshombe-bag, which will soon be converted into a shroud.

The main difference right now between the Northern and Southern Negro is that in the South the fight is still for equal rights, civil rights, etc., whereas in the North, the black man already has seen the bad faith of these terms, and has realized now for a long time that these rights we are asked to move toward are less than abstract rhetoric. Last summer the Northern urban industrial towns popped like mean firecrackers hooked up from ghetto to ghetto. Perhaps next summer these firecrackers will grow even larger—and it was largely in the North, where presumably all these civil rights, etc., have been attained, where these most recent demonstrations against white law have taken place. In the South the madness of the oppressors and their stupid henchmen, the poor white, is completely out in the open, the lines already clearly drawn. In the North, because of the lies and chicanery of the Northern industrialist's social form, the lines may seem less clearly drawn, the oppressor's hand more heavily veiled, but because of this veil, an even heavier sense of frustration incites the black man to anger. In the South you know the landscape is for real, in the North they try to tell you it's not. It is the added weight of being lied to, on top of every other indignity, that makes it all so hard to take. And then some white man hearing about oppressed Negroes on television will ask you for a little rational conversation on the subject. This will be a man (this hypothetical questioner) who probably does not know that policemen are menacing subhumans, whose socio-cultural conditioning—because they are usually grandsons of immigrants, *i.e.*, poor whites—has usually prepared them to hate niggers even before they get the official instructions (like James Bond) that they are "licensed to kill." The American policeman is the foulest social category in the world today, whether domestic, *e.g.*, "New York's Finest," or international (Humanitarians dropping out of the clouds, etc.).

You may see a barefoot South Carolina Negro, just grinning quietly—you wonder what's in behind those tired eyes—or you see another man just walking along, outwardly desolate, hands jammed deep in his pockets, and again you wonder, knowing and not knowing. Or you see a scene in Harlem or Bedford Stuyvesant, and know, that even in the North, the ghettoes (compounds) duplicate the South, and only add new frustrations not unlike the old. Sitting on garbage cans, thinking, or sleeping on benches, dreaming, or even pushing those "Jewish airplanes" in the garment center, grown men doing what they call a boy's job, but then still get sharp on weekends and go out hunting foxes. Blind anger sometimes in Georgia or the Bronx; staring at its image will set you off again, thinking of all these strong sweet people, their joy, even of those old hip black moles of men whose only conspicuous association with this century is a button that says, "I am registered, are you?"

What we would see in any realistic photo essay of America would be the image, pinpoints of light which show us the running sore called America. There is hope though, hope in some faces. Even the very young (the boys marching with their signs, the screaming little girls) know what it's all about. A sign says "Everybody wants Freedom." But what is the hope? What can it be? (America will not change because a few blacks and whites can kiss each other, or because Michael Schwerner or Andrew Goodman get themselves murdered. Most of the white kids who go into the South are only trying to save America or save themselves in America; there is more than enough guilt to go round. But there are people all over the world who don't want to see it saved.) Like I was asking, what is the hope? I say if your hope is for the survival of this society, this filthy order, no good. You lose. The hope is that young blacks will remember all of their lives what they are seeing, what they are witness to just by being alive and black in America, and that eventually they will use this knowledge scientifically, and erupt like Mt. Vesuvius to crush in hot lava these willful maniacs who call themselves white Americans.

the revolutionary theatre

The Revolutionary Theatre should force change; it should be change. (All their faces turned into the lights and you work on them black nigger magic, and cleanse them at having seen the ugliness. And if the beautiful see themselves, they will love themselves.) We are preaching virtue again, but by that to mean NOW, toward what seems the most constructive use of the world.

The Revolutionary Theatre must EXPOSE! Show up the insides of these humans, look into black skulls. White men will cower before this theatre because it hates them. Because they themselves have been trained to hate. The Revolutionary Theatre must hate them for hating. For presuming with their technology to deny the supremacy of the Spirit. They will all die because of this.

The Revolutionary Theatre must teach them their deaths. It must crack their faces open to the mad cries of the poor. It must teach them about silence and the truths lodged there. It must kill any God anyone names except Common Sense. The Revolutionary Theatre should flush the fags and murders out of Lincoln's face.

It should stagger through our universe correcting, insulting, preaching, spitting craziness—but a craziness taught to us in our most rational moments. People must be taught to trust true scientists (knowers, diggers, odd-balls) and that the holiness of life is the constant possi-bility of widening the consciousness. And they must be incited to strike back against *any* agency that attempts to prevent this widening.

The Revolutionary Theatre must Accuse and Attack anything that can be accused and attacked. It must Ac-cuse and Attack because it is a theatre of Victims. It looks at the sky with the victims' eyes, and moves the victims to look at the strength in their minds and their bodies.

Clay, in *Dutchman*, Ray in *The Toilet*, Walker in *The Slave*, are all victims. In the Western sense they could be heroes. But the Revolutionary Theatre, even if it is Western, must be anti-Western. It must show horrible coming attractions of *The Crumbling of the West*. Even as Artaud designed *The Conquest of Mexico*, so we must de-sign *The Conquest of White Eye*, and show the missionaries and wiggly liberals dying under blasts of concrete. For sound effects, wild screams of joy, from all the peoples of the world.

The Revolutionary Theatre must take dreams and give them a reality. It must isolate the ritual and histori-cal cycles of reality. But it must be food for all those who need food, and daring propaganda for the beauty of the Human Mind. It is a political theatre, a weapon to help in the slaughter of these dim-witted fatbellied white guys who somehow believe that the rest of the world is here for them to slobber on.

This should be a theatre of World Spirit. Where the spirit can be shown to be the most competent force in the world. Force. Spirit. Feeling. The language will be anybody's, but tightened by the poet's backbone. And even the language must show what the facts are in this consciousness epic, what's happening. We will talk about the world, and the preciseness with which we are able to summon the world will be our art. Art is method. And art, "like any ashtray or senator," remains in the world. Wittgenstein said ethics and aesthetics are one. I believe this. So the Broadway theatre is a theatre of reaction whose ethics, like its aesthetics, reflect the spiritual values of this unholy society, which sends young crackers all over the world blowing off colored people's heads. (In some of these flippy Southern towns they even shoot up the immigrants' Favorite Son, be it Michael Schwerner or JFKennedy.)

The Revolutionary Theatre is shaped by the world, and moves to reshape the world, using as its force the natural force and perpetual vibrations of the mind in the world. We are history and desire, what we are, and what any experience can make us.

It is a social theatre, but all theatre is social theatre. But we will change the drawing rooms into places where real things can be said about a real world, or into smoky rooms where the destruction of Washington can be plotted. The Revolutionary Theatre must function like an incendiary pencil planted in Curtis Lemay's cap. So that when the final curtain goes down brains are splattered over the seats and the floor, and bleeding nuns must wire SOS's to Belgians with gold teeth.

Our theatre will show victims so that their brothers in the audience will be better able to understand that they are the brothers of victims, and that they themselves are victims if they are blood brothers. And what we show must cause the blood to rush, so that pre-revolutionary temperaments will be bathed in this blood, and it will cause their deepest souls to move, and they will find themselves tensed and clenched, even ready to die, at what the soul has been taught. We will scream and cry, murder, run through the streets in agony, if it means some soul will be moved, moved to actual life understanding of what the world is, and what it ought to be. We are preaching virtue and feeling, and a natural sense of the self in the world. All men live in the world, and the world ought to be a place for them to live.

What is called the imagination (from image, magi, magic, magician, etc.) is a practical vector from the soul. It stores all data, and can be called on to solve all our "problems." The imagination is the projection of ourselves past our sense of ourselves as "things." Imagination (Image) is all possibility, because from the image, the initial circumscribed energy, any use (idea) is possible. And so begins that image's use in the world. Possibility is what moves us.

The popular white man's theatre like the popular white man's novel shows tired white lives, and the problems of eating white sugar, or else it herds bigcaboosed blondes onto huge stages in rhinestones and makes believe they are dancing or singing. WHITE BUSINESSMEN OF THE WORLD, DO YOU WANT TO SEE PEOPLE REALLY DANCING AND SINGING??? ALL OF YOU GO UP TO HARLEM AND GET YOURSELF KILLED. THERE WILL BE DANCING AND SINGING, THEN, FOR REAL!! (In *The Slave*, Walker Vessels, the black revolutionary, wears an armband, which is the insignia of the attacking army—a big red-lipped minstrel, grinning like crazy.)

The liberal white man's objection to the theatre of the revolution (if he is "hip" enough) will be on aesthetic grounds. Most white Western artists do not need to be "political," since usually, whether they know it or not, they are in complete sympathy with the most repressive social forces in the world today. There are more junior birdmen fascists running around the West today disguised as Artists than there are disguised as fascists. (But then, that word, *Fascist*, and with it, *Fascism*, has been made obsolete by the words *America*, and *Americanism*.) The American Artist usually turns out to be just a super-Bourgeois, because, finally, all he has to show for his sojourn through the world is "better taste" than the Bourgeois—many times not even that.

Americans will hate the Revolutionary Theatre because it will be out to destroy them and whatever they believe is real. American cops will try to close the theatres where such nakedness of the human spirit is paraded. American producers will say the revolutionary plays are filth, usually because they will treat human life as if it were actually happening. American directors will say that the white guys in the plays are too abstract and cowardly ("don't get me wrong . . . I mean aesthetically . . .") and they will be right.

The force we want is of twenty million spooks storming America with furious cries and unstoppable weapons. We want actual explosions and actual brutality: AN EPIC IS CRUMBLING and we must give it the space and hugeness of its actual demise. The Revolutionary Theatre, which is now peopled with victims, will soon begin to be peopled with new kinds of heroes—not the weak Hamlets debating whether or not they are ready to die for what's on their minds, but men and women (and minds) digging out from under a thousand years of "high art" and weak-faced dalliance. We must make an art that will function so as to call down the actual wrath of world spirit. We are witch doctors and assassins, but we will open a place for the true scientists to expand our consciousness. This is a theatre of assault. The play that will split the heavens for us will be called THE DESTRUCTION OF AMERICA. The heroes will be Crazy Horse, Denmark Vesey, Patrice Lumumba, and not history, not memory, not sad sentimental groping for a warmth in our despair; these will be new men, new heroes, and their enemies most of you who are reading this.

1965

american sexual reference: black male

M ost American white men are trained to be fags. For this reason it is no wonder their faces are weak and blank, left without the hurt that reality makes— anytime. That red flush, those silk blue faggot eyes. So white women become men-things, a weird combination, sucking the male juices to build a navel orange, which is themselves.

They are the "masters" of the world, and their children are taught this as God's fingerprint, so they can devote most of their energies to the nonrealistic, having no use for the real. They devote their energies to the nonphysical, the nonrealistic, and become estranged from them. Even their wars move to the stage where whole populations can be destroyed by *pushing a button*; but even so the paradox, which is the recurrence of the homosexual-motif underpinning to the society, is that the bomb, which is their constant threat and claim to manhood, is not even real. I mean, the elements that will make final the destruction of North America don't even have to worry about the bomb, since it is in the very areas North America is most vulnerable, Africa, Vietnam, Latin America, etc., where nuclear bombs are *obsolete*. And the General Staff, Defense Department, etc., all have realized this for quite some time. They also realize that North American (NATO-SEATO) armies can win almost no major war with conventional weapons. The Chinese or the Russians would run them back across the ice into those weird caves of their species' childhood.

The nonrealistic, the nonphysical. Think now, the goal of white society is luxury. Work is done by unfortunates. The purer white, the more estranged from, say, actual physical work. Who lifts the boards and steel, who does the hardest, stupidest, most brutalizing work? The reason the immigrants remain half-tough is that they must at least have certain black-sheep relatives still paving streets or working on the girders or heaving the garbage cans. But just as the Irish boxer has disappeared, and the Jewish boxer before him, now the Italian boxer is disappearing, and all the other shades of central Europe are now also cut out from any connection as performer with the "manly art." The Italians are managers, or train to be. The toughest Irish are the cops, etc., the law enforcers; ditto, the Italians who have one up on the Irish since they still have mobs, where violence, or the threat of violence, is always necessary. But they have to at least look like they could really do somebody harm. Can you, for a second, imagine the average middle-class white man able to do somebody harm? Alone? Without the technology that at this moment still has him rule the world? Do you understand the softness of the white man, the weakness, and again the estrangement from reality?

But change is the only constant in the world. Many times reversal of what already exists. So reason on this: that the newest of American weapons shoots darts. Guerilla warfare is the newest threat to the White Eyes, and the bomb won't work—only darts, and knives, and indigenous stealth. Guerilla/Gorilla; and the white man has always spoken of the nonwhite as monkeys, apes, gorillas.

Manhood is deemed the ability to oppress by the white man. At least, one is more of a man in the sense of being self-sufficient, able to provide for yourself and your family. The last words in an early pre-romance Yerby story spoken by a black soldier after his wife is outraged by white men is, simply, "I ain't no man." That is, I cannot provide, or protect.

Estrangement, alienation, are words to characterize the Euro-American intellectuals. This is the way the most perceptive of the twentieth century white intellectuals have characterized themselves, from Joyce to William Burroughs; and Sartre has uttered the most moving political pronouncement of the white man's alienation. Finally, it is an alienation from the *real* that is meant, because, as the formal intellectuals would have it, one has found something more meaningful than reality (but what could that be? and could it really exist, apart from reality?), which would be God, or cult, whether royalist or beatnik. The most sensitive white men have always claimed not to have any part in white Euro-American culture-results. They have always decried its unfeeling materialism and murderous assertions of self-sufficiency. Sartre, for instance, realizes that one of the concomitant features of white culture, as it has existed since the Greeks, is to make victims, and then, to top that, to convince or try to convince these victims that they are better off shackled to the white man's notions of what the world is, even though those notions justify their existence as victims.

This alienation syndrome is most pronounced in the sensitive, the artists, etc., because what they claim as motive for their lives they try to understand as being separate from the rest of the culture. This kind of thinking leads to ludicrous spectacles like a white middle-class man growing a beard and wearing sandals, etc., or staring out the window in weak-drugged contemplation, claiming he is somehow *not* what the rest of the white North Americans are. Yet most of these artists, intellectuals, etc., are exactly what their culture predicts and produces, in fact they are the concentrate of it, given a more glorious appearance in the world by the heavy disguise of "art." I mean the average white American artist believes the world is socio-economically cool, it is just that "people have such bad taste," etc. The strong phrase in defense of this attitude is always, "I keep out of politics."

But for a man to be living in a certain social order, in fact, to have benefited by that order (and the filth of its image) and yet claim to have no connection with it, is unrealistic in the extreme. The artist is the concentrate, as I said, of the society's tendencies—the extremist. And the most extreme form of alienation acknowledged within white society is homosexuality. The long abiding characterization of the Western artist as usually "queer" does not seem out of place.

White North American culture is committed to the idea of individualism, ego-satisfaction, and personal gain. "Free enterprise," an old white man with drooping eyes will tell you. And he will mean individualism, ego-satisfaction and personal gain—at the world's expense. It is unrealistic to think of the world as a place where some people should live in one manner, supported by the labor of the majority of the world's peoples. Not only is this thinking unrealistic, but by the exclusivity of its form (and E.X.C.L.U.S.I.V.E. is the word dead-loined white ladies cherish most) it also isolates the white man from the most common realities of the planet, so that most often his concerns seem stupid, fake and abstract, on one simple level. In recent times he has never had to be really concerned, even terrified, by the *basic* issues of living—eating, gainful employment, shelter—I mean on a level where these things, these necessities, might easily not be forthcoming, where, in fact, these things might be impossible fantasies. The kind of wish-fulfillment fantasies that reinforce the harshness of the poor man's reality.

The black man in America, as well as most of the world's colored people (which are most of the world's people, some 87 per cent), are what the white man calls "underprivileged," *i.e.*, they cannot move through their lives with the easy confidence white luxury provides. But luxury reinforces weakness; a people who lose their self-sufficiency because they depend on their "subjects" to do the world's work become effeminate and perverted. (Talk about "Greek Love," Roman decadence, and the fop-dandy style that has strung itself out as the "cultural" background of this society. And over the years even the hero image of the white American has changed to where most of the heroes, leading men, etc., on television or in the movies, at least look like out-and-out fairies.)

Now these fairies are showing up as CIA agents and spies, reflecting the needs and temperament of the Euro-American. Licensed to Kill is their special nut, which they exercise in real life in most parts of the world, *e.g.*, Vietnam. But the CIA agent is the hero, a man who travels all over the world subverting governments and murdering the white man's enemies. James Bond (Napoleon Solo, etc.) is the perfect white man of the mid 60's: suave, jaded, *licensed to kill*—a murdering gadgeteer.

The black man in America has always been expected to function as less than a man; this was taken for granted, and was the ugliest weight of his enslavement. The liberal white man has always promised the de-testicled black some progress to manhood. In other words, "We will let your balls grow back . . . one day! Just be cool."

In slavery times, theoretically, the slave master could make it with any black woman he could get to. The black man was powerless to do anything to prevent it; many times he was even powerless to keep his woman with him, or his children. One effect of this largely one-sided "integration" was to create a very deep hatred and suspicion in the black man for any black woman who had dealings with white men. This is a feeling that still exists.

On the other hand, the black man and the white woman were not supposed to have any connections, even in anybody's wildest fantasies. This was (is?) the great taboo of the society. This taboo did a number of things. For one, it created for such a possible blackman-whitewoman union an aura of mystery and wild sensuality that could provoke either principal to investigate, if either were intrepid or curious enough.

The reason the white woman was supposed to be intrigued by the black man was because he was basic and elemental emotionally (which is true for the non-brainwashed black, simply because there is no reason he should not be; the black man is more "natural" than the white simply because he has fewer *things* between him and reality, fewer wrappers, fewer artificial rules), therefore "wilder," harder, and almost insatiable in his lovemaking.

The reasons the black man was drawn to the white woman, I think, were quite different. There has never been any large currency, to my knowledge, for any rumor that white women were better bed partners than black, as a matter of fact the myth has always preached quite the opposite. But there was a social beatification to the gray lady, which issued from certain aspects of the situation. One aspect is, of course, the wildly "protective" attitude white society has for The White Woman, as far as copulating with a black man is concerned. Also, because of this protective (defensive) odor the white man spread around the white woman, she became, in a sense, one of the most significant acquisitions of white society for a certain kind of black man. But this is generally true even for the white man. The glorification and foolishness of white ladyness in the mainstream culture is notorious. Even white homosexual poets speak of The Lady, who is generally *never* supposed to be popped, by nobody. Which is stupid. (Even think back to medieval mores, and the cult of Lady who was never "sullied," and the knights who always practiced coitus interruptus to show their chivalry; or the white church Virgin who gave birth to the truth, without being touched by human hands.) Glamour girls, movie stars, mysterious love parts, selling toothpaste, cigarettes, or atom bombs—put a white lady next to it, and you bet it'll sell. The billboards wouldn't lie to you. Although I will add here that the Miss America contest proposes for its vision of American White Ladies that they are the ugliest on the planet.

The image I get is of a dumpy, but somehow seductive, strongwhore who waddles around the house in expensive cosmetics. Ask somebody what are all those coats of paint and powder for, and they will tell you to make them beautiful, which is what they will tell you about, say, their serious literature, *i.e.*, all those layers of fake artifice are for the beauty that is to keep the thing away from them, that is to keep it, like Negroes, cool, and themselves undisturbable since their filthy enterprises need, for certain, most of their attention. The white man doesn't have time for reality, the white woman uses her leisure to cover it up.

Mixed marriages, etc., take place usually among the middle class of one kind or another—usually the "liberated" segment of the middle class, artists, bohemians, entertainers, or the otherwise "famous." (Liberated here meaning that each member has somehow gotten at least superficially free of his history. For the black man this would mean that he has grown, somehow, less black; for the white woman it means, at one point, that she has more liberal opinions, or at least likes to bask in the gorgeousness of being a hip, ok, sophisticated, outcast. There is a whole social grouping of white women who are body-missionaries, and feel themselves *elevated* through such acts as would qualify them as either "swingin' chicks" or strong women, in a land of women who are, as Ezra Pound said awhile back, "Like a skein of loose silk blown against a wall . . . dying piece-meal of a sort of emotional anemia." This is what's known, in the West, as being ladylike.)

For the black man, acquisition of a white woman always signified some special power the black man had managed to obtain (illicitly, therefore with a sweeter satisfaction) within white society. It was also a way of participating more directly in white society. One very heavy entrance into White America. (No matter if any of these directions said "Love.")

The innumerable rape scenes "reported" in the South and the North of white women by black men, whether all true or not, still propose a wild emotional state for such liaisons just by virtue of their telling. (They say a lot of women *want* to be raped! But by a black man??? That's pretty far out . . . and scary?) The most heinous crime against white society would be just that, the rape, the taking forcibly of one of whitie's treasures. This is one pole. There is also, one must suppose, the simple fact of opposing exoticisms (white thighs rub against black; something like a Franz Kline).

In the marginal middle-class societies where inter-popping exists at a higher rate than in most of the U.S. (though, for certain, there are handyman-housewife relationships and others that go on, believe it, even in those whitest—or blackest—parts of the South), these relationships take on special significance. Trading experience in bohemia and near-cults, black people earn their keep by trading in their ghetto or "other life" experiences, and that phrase *trading in* should be taken both ways—extensions of cultures, plain miscegenation are the orders of the day. But also, there seems to be a softening of the black man or woman, as I implied, through such connections with the morally weaker white element, merely through the introduction of luxury, finally spiritual, and the changing of attitudes. In this sense integration is assimilation and the permission to see the world suddenly through mealy ofay eyes.

But it is interesting that the black man in these intellectually "liberated" environments is one of the strongest shaping forces upon those environments, bearing the thickest life forces, even to the point where his woes are famous, his need for violence both fact and legend. And this is so even though the liberation, the "transcending," of his social sources, makes for a kind of wilder domestication than the straightup black bourgeois, but it is a domestication, nevertheless. It is a domestication because no matter that the strong black boys walk their various bohemias, or near bohemias, or hip university scenes, like cowboys, full of beguiling stories about their former existences as underprivileged (*i.e.*, before they, like, discovered ART, or THE WHITE THIGH, or some kind of uncommon existence as con-man or hustler or know-it-all), which lend a kind of honest drama to their lives, in distinct contrast to most of the residents of said liberated areas whose dramas you can see any night on television. The black man is weakened by any friend-contact with whites simply because his concerns will shift (if he is "influenced") and the raw problems of survival—mindsoulbody—will be obfuscated, and re-placed by unwhite hallucinations. That is, such a black man can be taught, by his new environment, to imitate the needs of people who have not the same sources as he, who have not the same needs, who, finally, are the same white people whose murders are being plotted by 90 per cent of the world, though they come on as super-feelers or Artists, or as not having anything to do with "what the Government is doing."

But these liberated zones of America are surely the closest mockups of North American Utopia going. That is, they come closest to pretending some kind of egali-tarian society. And in this context, though finally it is worse than false, the swaggering black boys who move confidently through such societies, with an absolute certainty as to their worth as "intellectuals" (meaning "members of the community"), move with each strength-ening of these cultural connections with the community, further and further away from the strongest emotional reference in their lives, their blackness. (Which is the final radical quality in social America.)

So the fake egalitarian society backs the young black man away from his blackness by providing a false bridge of mutual interest (call it Art, or the tweaking of belly hairs early mornings by some sad product of America) between himself and a more interesting variety of white liberalism.

What makes this imagined *détente* between black and white attractive to the black man is usually his belief that he has actually transcended his social history, and entered a world of pure light, etc. Also, there is a certain "superiority" of reference that black man can make—as I said, those tales of another, harsher, life—and a reference to values enforced by a grimmer reality, which, of course, seem more valid simply because they were imposed by cold street necessity, rather than abstract intellectualization. (Interesting too is the observation that the single Negro in such circumstances *is* exotic, ditto his history, and "fading" needs; but more than one, or maybe, wow, a group of blacks is not no more any cute thing, but frankly depressing.)

So integration is, again, merely whitening to fit the white soul's image. It is also, for the black man, a weakening, through contact with a beatified decadence. There is, for instance, the stud role the black man can assume in these "liberalized" portions of the American mind. The black man is covered with sex smell, gesture, aura, because, for one reason, the white man has tried to keep the black man hidden the whole time he has been in America. These were heathens that were brought over in the slave ships, or savages, or animals, they were—are you kidding?—definitely not men, not human. And when the possibility arose that these animals really might be men, then the ballcutting ceremony was trotted out immediately, just to make sure that these would-be men wouldn't try any funnystuff (especially not with the realmen's old ladies).

So the white man has tried to cover black people's humanity, to make it easier on himself whilst running his businesses. And when you cover another man's humanity, his humanness, his being, then you cover that part of your own which would respond to the ex-man's humanity had you allowed him to keep it. But the stud role, which is joke/myth/conditional fact of a kind of Negro role within these liberalized communities, is a vector from straightup America as well. In the various bohemias and nearbohemias there is a kind of openness about the white man's (and woman's) needs, hence such normally hidden or reversed image of the black man as superstud for white women (as that image is projected by both black and white) is not only given large currency, but taken literally by both black and white. In straightup America this role is reversed, for obvious reasons. Here the black man is called rapist, where even the rolling of his eyes can get him in trouble. That is, the average ofay thinks of the black man as potentially raping every white lady in sight. Which is true, in the sense that the black man should want to rob the white man of everything he has.

In the bohemias, etc., where fantasies are given play as "new" ways of life, many black men do work out this robbery (rape) motif, even though the objects of such psychodramas unfailingly give their "permission." Just the same, the hip white boy will run some local girl down because "She's got this thing for spades, man . . . only cats she makes it with . . ." etc., and there is only disdain in his voice. And where the "big black muscular beasts of unbelievable passion" story is laughed at by the liberated ofay, it still rests heavy and stinging in his consciousness as a definite affront.

But for most whites the guilt of the robbery is the

guilt of the rape. That is, they know in their deepest hearts that they *should* be robbed, and the white woman understands that only in the rape sequence is she likely to get cleanly, viciously popped, which is a thing her culture provides for only in fantasies of "evil." But then, the white man has never reunderstood the sex act since the dissociation of childbirth was made. The puritanical excesses of the White Eyes who call the procreative act (or thought of it as) "evil" are only compensation for their lack of couth in handling the world's business. I mean for one thousand years the White Eye has killed people for his luxury; as the killing increased, and the cover stories grew more fixed, and the possibility of reform (among the white men, *i.e.*, that they get themselves together and try to be human beings) lessened, the withdrawal from sex as *creation* grew more extreme. Sex was *dirty*, because first of all it meant a nakedness that could not be supported, because men surrounded and grown fat on evil cannot envision themselves as *naked*, *i.e.*, completely seen, except in a vision of terror, hence evil. Also there was/is in the white man's unconscious, in response to his own evil, the desire not to create himself again, a definite anti-regenerative drive. (Let us say it is nature's way of cutting down on destructive species.) And when the white man speaks of population explosion, he means the nonwhite plotters more than himself, and he is really only running down a very sophisticated plea for genocide.

The black man, then, because he can enter into the sex act with less guilt as to its results, is freer. Because of the robbery/rape syndrome, the black man will *take* the white woman in a way that does not support the myth of The Lady, thus springing an outside reality that will seem either beast-like or God-like, depending on the lady's psychological connection with White American Crime.

But also, the "liberated" white man is more aware of his culture's deficiencies and ugliness. The beatnik longs for experience he understands is missing from his reality. Jack Kerouac's virtuous, mysterious, sensual black is drawn from his conscious/unconscious understanding that the white man is in evil withdrawal from the sweetest feelings in life. The beatnik or white Negro, as Mailer called them, wants out of the mainstream ofay world, and sees the Negro as the image of such alienation. There is a white boy Negroes on the Lower Eastside call Superspade, in honor of his dedication. The imitation of certain aspects of black culture by these whites makes that fake bridge of common concern seem even realer.

The white man's concern for the black man's sexual habits is so obsessive that in mainstream public images of the black man (e.g., movies, etc.) he is always made to seem as if sex would never never come into his mind. It is only recently that any currency has been given in the mass media to the idea that a black man and a black woman might actually feel sexually attracted to each other. "Avant garde" movies and musicals anxious to be controversial will now even imply that white woman-black man could possibly get together, some kind of way.

The black man as robber/rapist (take it further, it is "murderer"), any talk of "social progress" to the contrary, inhabits a constant place in the white American psyche, much like the place Sonny Liston was made to come to life in, in the white press. Sonny was given the "nigger in the alleyway with a blackjack" casting, which, finally, is true, and admirable. But the actual social image of the black man in America is so warped for the white man sealed in his own lust, and guilt (that madness drives them to do wild things), that all he sees is his own twisted countenance smeared stupidly over all the world. And for that reason there are niggers in alleyways, etc., all over the world, waiting to do in each and every white man the devil creates.

When I was about nine my grandmother told me a story about Alabama. She said that one time these white men had taken this young boy, about seventeen or so, and cut his "privates" off, and then, my grandmother said, "they stuffed 'um in his mouth." And some men, she said, grabbed her, and made her watch. The boy who was murdered was a "rapist." He had probably been called, in one way or another; maybe the woman's clitoris was trembling so, it banged loudly against the sides of her soul. And cheap drama is one thing white women live on. But however she drew him to her, and he drew her, toward his thing, the mutilation characterizes the white man's insane fear of black creation. And the meattool of its physical manifestation is something to be destroyed. (Movies, liberals, etc., just think it out of existence. As I said, they treat the black man as if he would never have any use for sex, *e.g.*, the classic frightened coons of The Great American Cinema.) But the white man of almost any persuasion has a deadly concern for the black man's sex—usually this concern is shown through mutilation—whether in the honest concerns of the class of white men who lynch, that is to say, actually cut the organs off, or in the hardly more subtle way of public liberal deballing.

But the mutilation of the sex organs occurs again and again during lynchings. It is not enough that the black man has been socially demanned; the actual rite must go on too. And the act of cutting off a man's sex organs and stuffing them in his mouth should be analyzed as closely and deeply as possible. By removing the black man's organs, his manness, the white man removes the threat of the black man asserting that manness, by taking the white man's most prized possession. Trying to strangle a man with his own sex organs, his own manhood: that is what white America has always tried to do to the black man—make him swallow his manhood.

But the white man's attitude toward sex in general is diseased. Because of his unconscious reluctance to reproduce himself the white man must make sex dirty. (It is in the "individualistic" ego-oriented society that homosexuality flourishes most since the Responsibility of bearing one's generations is not present among the kind of decadent middle class such a society creates.)

The so-called morality of white American Society and the seriousness with which this morality is supposed to be held (like when they bust some movie or book because it's obscene, i.e., that it should be kept off the scene, like the Greeks said of Aeschylus' *The Persians*, because it offends that morality or terrifies it) are a great part of the fantasy life that enables the Western white man to justify all of his murders and perversion as serving a greater good. But this good is a mirror of ice reflecting only himself. The world is made for him, and the things on it.

And in this morality, this placement of himself in the world, any mention of what actually happens in the world is at least controversial. If it is exact, it is liable to be also obscene. To be kept off the scene, lest it expose some unwitting American to the whole planet's woes, and he be wheeled face to face with some aspect of his society's decay. The American cannot believe that he is a cancer. But he dies of cancer, and heart trouble. The madly spreading virus, and the organism suddenly heart/less.

Morality, like mores, means custom, what is usually done, what is subscribed to. White Americans are, as they like to think of themselves, great moralists. The Western white man has the morality of a primitive meat eater living in the snow, afraid that the world has not provided enough food for *all* people to survive. The white man is a primitive, and his sexual understanding is that of a primitive.

The white man is a primitive because he is turned backwards, and all his emotional allegiances are toward the static, the "unchanging," but all is change, and things that cannot change die out. The white man is a primitive because all the rest of the world's peoples must think toward the future, toward *change*, because they must have it.

Men are made to think and feel. They are not made to live the way the white man has made them live. The cycle of world spirit has always predicted the final emancipation of man from illusion and pain. The stupidest work in the universe man has already learned to do away with. Now, the one thing left to do is to remove the obstructions from man's path. The white man, at this point in history, is the major obstruction on the path of man's progress. The white man will not change, but he will be changed by the force of world spirit—into ashes.

The white man is in love with the past, with dead things, and soon he will become one. He is in love with the past because it is in the past that he really exists. He understands that he cannot possibly exist in the future, or even in the present. For instance with the idea of art, what is done now, in the present, or with presage of some stronger future, is always treated shabbily by mainstream white society, for one reason because it makes reference to living humanity, which is always threatening to what is "established." The white man worships the artifact; his museums are full of dead things, artifacts, which at best can only make reference to life. But the stupidity is not in keeping the artifacts, which all societies do, and should do to better understand the various roads that man has come along, it is the worship of these artifacts, these dead things, that is finally evil. The worship of these dead things, in opposition to things which are alive.

The white man must fear things that are alive, because he senses they will replace him. Life and creation (of life) are equally terrifying to him. (The stuffing of the genitals into the mouth . . . think about that . . . making a man destroy his powers to create, destroying his seed, and his generations.)

Black creation terrifies the white man, because it is strong, ubiquitous. The white man is like the land, so minute in the world, so in danger from the raging sea, which sweeps the world into any shape it wills. Black creation is as strong as black flesh. If the raped white woman has a child (or the raped black one) it is a black child. The black woman can bring forth nothing out of her womb but blackness, the black man can send out no other kind of seed. And that seed, anywhere, makes black.

The black shows through, and is genetically dominant. The white race will disappear simply enough in genetic time, which cannot be separated from the context of its happening, *i.e.*, social facts which make the genetically weaker whites dangerous in the world, as well as actually diseased. (As the dying apple in a barrel is *socially* dangerous, since in its spreading, disease can wipe out the entire apple society.)

The white man calls the mulatto black. And senses that in "assimilation" the white race would disappear, simply. So the white man's disgust at the thought of the black man hitting on his stuff.

But in the white man's sexual life is found the exact replica of his conscious, unconscious, social life. Reich has written about the repression of sexuality in the white man, and how this blocking of natural emission and other violent energies causes cancer and madness or white Americans. And this sexual energy is a dirtiness, an ecstasy, which always threatens the "order" *i.e.*, "rationalism," the ahumane asexual social order the white man seeks with all his energies to uphold.

There are wild areas of *self*-negation in the sexual experience. That is, a selfless identification with energy. But white men are first of all Selves and Egos and this is their only identity; as *anti-spirits*. They have no other place in the world.

blackhope*

In a time of chaos, in a time of trouble, we're asking for unity, black unity as defense against these mad white people who continue to run the world.

These same mad white people who are killing black unity and black people all over the world, in Africa, Asia, Latin America, these same mad white people who every day of our lives demonstrate that they are not fit to live on the same planet with soulful human beings, these are the enemies of our world, these are the fiends against whom we black people had better protect ourselves.

And we must begin to protect ourselves against every aspect of the white man's thinking. Because his thinking is aimed at destroying us, or reducing us to pitiful objects known as "Negroes." And everybody knows what "Negroes" are; strait-jacketed lazy clowns, whose only joy is carrying out the white man's will.

But there are some of us who will not be Negroes, who know that indeed we are something else, something stronger . . . there are some of us who know we are black people, and that we have been forced for the last few centuries to live and slave for maniacs in the worst insane asylum in man's history.

Knowing all this, we black people should be *at least* suspicious of everything coming out of a white man's

* Speech given in front of the Hotel Theresa as Director of The Black Arts Repertory Theatre.

mouth. Whether he is talking to you in an appliance store (telling you about the wonders of "36 months to pay") or from the fake respectability of his television stations, radio stations or lying newspapers. I am telling you it is very dangerous to believe anything the white man tells you . . . you know his record . . . especially if he wants you to believe it.

And also because black people have, and must realize that we have, our own standards and references for judging the world. And we must begin to make use of them, and regard what the white man says as dealing with another reality, because we know, we black people know, what our own reality is. Look out your window, or into your heart, you know who and where you are. You know what you feel. You know what you have to do!!!! And let no white man or imitation white man tell you different.

So now we read in the *Herald Tribune* or the colored people's uptown version of the *Herald Tribune* that, as usual, black people cannot manage their affairs without the kindly old missionaries' help. And that help turns out to be arrogant gangster cops and crew-cut robots from Washington. As usual!! What is it about the white man that he cannot do any business anywhere in the world, especially not with colored peoples, except it be at gunpoint? Now they are storming into the Black Community waving their guns asking to see the books. No book a black man could get together would ever satisfy these aliens. Because all they want, ever, from the black man, is his life.

Black People, do not be fooled by these devils. Do not let them destroy Haryou-Act or any other project designed to help black people. Do not be fooled into letting the white man kill you and your children by letting him destroy those agencies that would save you. Do not let them tear out your hearts with their lies and contempt. Do not let them smear our leaders, do not let them enter into this community with their bullshit integration fairytales. Remember, you are at war with the devil himself. And the devil, and everybody knows this, will do anything to suck up another soul.

So now we are asking for unity, a black unity, in every place where there are black people. We are asking for a massive unity. A coming together of Brothers and Sisters to enter in service against the devil.

Black People we must at last come together to protect ourselves and what we love. In each block, in each house, in each black heart. All these groups, organizations, viewpoints, religions, had better come together, agreed on one term, that they are black people, and that they are tired of being weak slaves. We are asking for a unity so strong that it will shake up the world. We are asking for all black people to come on in now, and lock arms against these beasts. We must unify. We *must* have unity. We must use our strength and minds against our enemies not against each other.

If you want a new world, Brothers and Sisters, if you want a world where you can all be beautiful human beings, we must throw down our differences and come together as black people. And once we have done this, you know for yourself, there is no force on earth that can harm or twist us. No devil left in creation to mess up the world.

the legacy of malcolm x,
and the coming of the black nation

1

The reason Malik was killed (the reasons) is because he was thought dangerous by enough people to allow and sanction it. Black People and white people.

Malcolm X was killed because he was dangerous to America. He had made too great a leap, in his sudden awareness of *direction* and the possibilities he had for influencing people, anywhere.

Malcolm was killed because he wanted to become official, as, say, a statesman. Malcolm wanted an effective form in which to enrage the white man, a practical form. And he had begun to find it.

For one thing, he'd learned that Black Conquest will be a *deal*. That is, it will be achieved through deals as well as violence. (He was beginning through his African statesmanship to make deals with other nations, as statesman from a *nation*. An oppressed Black Nation "laying" in the Western Hemisphere.)

This is one reason he could use the "universal" Islam— to be at peace with all dealers. The idea was to broaden, formalize, and elevate the will of the Black Nation so that it would be able to move a great many people and resources in a direction necessary to *spring* the Black Man.

"*The Arabs must send us guns or we will accuse them of having sold us into slavery!*" is international, and opens Black America's ports to all comers. When the ports are open, there is an instant *brotherhood of purpose* formed with most of the world.

Malcolm's legacy was his life. What he rose to be and through what channels, *e.g.*, Elijah Muhammad and the Nation of Islam, as separate experiences. Malcolm changed as a minister of Islam: under Elijah's tutelage, he was a different man—the difference being, between a man who is preaching Elijah Muhammad and a man who is preaching political engagement and, finally, national sovereignty. (Elijah Muhammad is now the second man, too.)

The point is that Malcolm had begun to call for Black National Consciousness. And moved this consciousness into the broadest possible arena, operating with it as of now. We do not want a Nation, we are a Nation. We must strengthen and formalize, and play the world's game with what we have, from where we are, as a *truly* separate people. America can give us nothing; all bargaining must be done by mutual agreement. But finally, terms must be given by Black Men *from their own shores*—which is where they live, where we all are, now. The land is literally ours. And we must begin to act like it.

The landscape should belong to the people who see it all the time.

We begin by being Nationalists. But a nation is land, and wars are fought over land. The sovereignty of nations, the sovereignty of culture, the sovereignty of race, the sovereignty of ideas and ways "into" the world.

The world in the twentieth century, and for some centuries before, is, literally, backward. The world can be understood through any idea. And the purely *social* condition of the world in this millennium, as, say, "compared" to other millennia, might show a far greater loss than gain, if this were not balanced by concepts and natural forces. That is, we think ourselves into the balance and ideas are necessarily "advanced" of what is simply here (*what's going on*, so to speak). And there are rockets and super cars. But, again, the loss? What might it have been if my people were turning the switches? I mean, these have been our White Ages, and all learning has suffered.

And so the Nationalist concept is the arrival of conceptual and environmental strength, or the realization of it in its totality by the Black Man in the West, *i.e.*, that he is not of the West, but even so, like the scattered Indians after movie cavalry attacks, must regroup, and return that force on a fat, ignorant, degenerate enemy.

We are a people. We are unconscious captives unless we realize this—that we have always been separate, except in our tranced desire to be the thing that oppressed us, after some generations of having been "programmed" (a word suggested to me by Jim Campbell and Norbert Wieners) into believing that our greatest destiny was to become white people!

2

Malcolm X's greatest contribution, other than to propose a path to internationalism and, hence, the entrance of the American Black Man into a world-wide allegiance against the white man (in most recent times he proposed to do it using a certain kind of white liberal as a lever), was to preach Black Consciousness to the Black Man. As a minister for the Nation of Islam, Malcolm talked about a black consciousness that took its form from religion. In his last days he talked of another black consciousness that proposed politics as its moving energy.

But one very important aspect of Malcolm's earlier counsels was his explicit call for a National Consciousness among Black People. And this aspect of Malcolm's philosophy certainly did abide throughout his days. The feeling that somehow the Black Man was different, as being, as a being, and finally, in our own time, as judge. And Malcolm propounded these differences as life anecdote and religious (political) truth and made the consideration of Nationalist ideas significant and powerful in our day.

Another very important aspect of Malcolm's earlier (or the Honorable Elijah Muhammad's) philosophy was the whole concept of land and land-control as central to any talk of "freedom" or "independence." The Muslim tack of asking for land within the continental United States in which Black People could set up their own nation, was given a special appeal by Malcolm, even though the request was seen by most people outside the movement as "just talk" or the amusing howls of a gadfly.

But the whole importance of this insistence on land is just now beginning to be understood. Malcolm said many times that when you speak about revolution you're talking about land—changing the ownership or usership of some specific land which you think is yours. But any talk of Nationalism also must take this concept of land

and its primary importance into consideration because, finally, any Nationalism which is not intent on restoring or securing autonomous space for a people, *i.e.*, a nation, is at the very least shortsighted.

Elijah Muhammad has said, "We want our people in America, whose parents or grandparents were descendants from slaves, to be allowed to establish a separate state or territory of their own—either on this continent or elsewhere. We believe that our former slave-masters are obligated to provide such land and that the area must be fertile and minerally rich." And the Black Muslims seem separate from most Black People because the Muslims have a National Consciousness based on their aspirations for land. Most of the Nationalist movements in this country advocate that that land is in Africa, and Black People should return there, or they propose nothing about land at all. It is impossible to be a Nationalist without talking about land. Otherwise, your Nationalism is a misnamed kind of "difficult" opposition to what the white man has done, rather than the advocation of another people becoming the rulers of themselves, and sooner or later the rest of the world.

The Muslims moved from the Back-to-Africa concept of Marcus Garvey (the first large movement by Black People back to a National Consciousness, which was, finally, only viable when the Black Man focused on Africa as literally "back home") to the concept of a Black National Consciousness existing in this land the Black captives had begun to identify as home. (Even in Garvey's time, there was not a very large percentage of Black People who really wanted to leave. Certainly, the newly emerging Black bourgeoisie would have nothing to do with "returning" to Africa. They were already created in the image of white people, as they still are, and wanted nothing to do with Black.

What the Muslims wanted was a profound change. The National Consciousness focused on actual (non-abstract) land, identifying a people, in a land where they lived. Garvey wanted to go back to Jordan. A real one. The Nation of Islam wanted Jordan closer. Before these two thrusts, the Black Man in America, as he was Christianized, believed Jordan was in the sky, like pie, and absolutely supernatural.

Malcolm, then, wanted to give the National Consciousness its political embodiment, and send it out to influence the newly forming third world, in which this consciousness was to be included. The concept of Blackness, the concept of the National Consciousness, the proposal of a political (and diplomatic) form for this aggregate of Black spirit, these are the things given to us by Garvey, through Elijah Muhammad, and finally given motion into still another area of Black response by Malcolm X.

Malcolm's legacy to Black People is what he moved toward, as the accretion of his own spiritual learning and the movement of Black People in general, through the natural hope, a rise to social understanding within the new context of the white nation and its decline under hypocrisy and natural "oppositeness" which has pushed all of us toward "new" ideas. We are all the products of national spirit and worldview. We are drawn by the vibrations of the entire nation. If there were no bourgeois Negroes, none of us would be drawn to that image. They, bourgeois Negroes, were shaped through the purposive actions of a national attitude, and finally, by the demands of a particular culture.

At which point we must consider what cultural attitudes are, what culture is, and what National Consciousness has to do with these, *i.e.*, if we want to understand what Malcolm X was pointing toward, and why the Black Man now must move in that direction since the world will not let him move any other way. The Black Man is possessed by the energies of historic necessity and the bursting into flower of a National Black Cultural Consciousness, and with that, in a living future, the shouldering to power of Black culture and, finally, Black Men . . . and then, Black ideals, which are different descriptions of a God. A righteous sanctity, out of which worlds are built.

3

What the Black Man must do now is look down at the ground upon which he stands, and claim it as his own. It is not abstract. Look down! Pick up the earth, or jab your fingernails into the concrete. It is real and it is yours, if you want it.

But to want it, as our own, is the present direction. To want what we are and where we are, but rearranged by our own consciousness. That is why it was necessary first to recrystallize national aspirations behind a Garvey. The Africans who first came here were replaced by Americans, or people responding to Western stimuli and then Americans. In order for the Americans to find out that they had come from another place, were, hence, alien, the Garvey times had to come. Elijah said we must have a place, to be, ourselves. Malcolm made it contemporarily secular.

So that now we must find the flesh of our spiritual creation. We must be *conscious*. And to be conscious is to be *cultured*, processed in specific virtues and genius. We must respond to this National Consciousness with our souls, and use the correspondence to come into our own.

The Black Man will always be frustrated until he has land (A Land!) of his own. All the thought processes and emotional orientation of "national liberation movements"—from slave uprisings onward—have always given motion to a Black National (and Cultural) Consciousness. These movements proposed that judgments were being made by Black sensibility, and that these judgments were *necessarily* different from those of the white sensibility—different, and after all is said and done, inimical.

Men are what their culture predicts (enforces). Culture is, simply, the way men live. How they have come to live. What they are formed by. Their total experience, and its implications and theories. Its paths.

The Black Man's paths are alien to the white man. Black Culture is alien to the white man. Art and religion are the results and idealized supernumeraries of culture. Culture in this sense, as Sapir said, is "The National Genius," whether it be a way of fixing rice or killing a man.

I said in *Blues People*: "Culture is simply how one lives and is connected to history by habit." Here is a graphic structure of the relationships and total context of culture:

The Axis (context and evoked relationships) of Culture

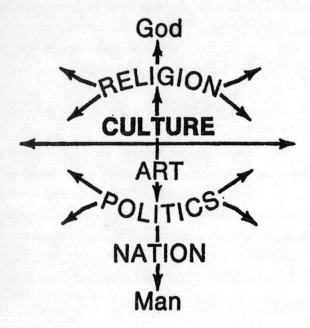

God is man idealized (humanist definition). Religion is the aspiration of man toward an idealized existence. An existence in which the functions of God and man are harmonious, even identical. Art is the movement forward, the understanding progress of man. It is feeling and making. A nation (social order) is made the way people *feel* it should be made. A face is too. Politics is man's aspiration toward an order. Religion is too. Art is an ordering as well. And all these categories are spiritual, but are also the result of the body, at one point, serving as a container of feeling. The soul is no less sensitive.

Nations are races. (In America, white people have become a nation, an identity, a race.) Political integration in America will not work because the Black Man is played on by special forces. His life, from his organs, *i.e.*, the life of the body, what it needs, what it wants, to become, is different—and for this reason racial is biological, finally. We are a different *species*. A species that is evolving to world power and philosophical domination of the world. The world will move the way Black People move!

If we take the teachings of Garvey, Elijah Muhammad and Malcolm X (as well as Frazier, DuBois and Fanon), we know for certain that the solution of the Black Man's problems will come only through Black National Consciousness. We also know that the focus of change will be racial. (If we *feel* differently, we have different *ideas*. Race is feeling. Where the body, and the organs, come in. Culture is the preservation of these feelings in superrational to rational form. Art is one method of expressing these feelings and identifying the form, as an emotional phenomenon.) In order for the Black Man in the West to absolutely know himself, it is necessary for him to see himself first as culturally separate from the white man. That is, to be conscious of this separation and use the strength it proposes.

Western Culture (the way white people live and think) is passing. If the Black Man cannot identify himself as separate, and understand what this means, he will perish along with Western Culture and the white man.

What a culture produces is, and refers to, is an image—a picture of a process, since it is a form of a process: movement seen. The changing of images, of references, is the Black Man's way back to the racial integrity of the captured African, which is where we must take ourselves, in feeling, to be truly the warriors we propose to be. To form an absolutely rational attitude toward West man, and West thought. Which is what is needed. To see the white man as separate and as enemy. To make a fight according to the absolute realities of the world as it is.

Good–Bad, Beautiful–Ugly, are all formed as the result of image. The mores, customs, of a place are the result of experience, and a common reference for defining it—common images. The three white men in the film *Gunga Din* who kill off hundreds of Indians, Greek hero-style, are part of an image of white men. The various black porters, gigglers, ghostchumps and punkish Indians, etc., that inhabit the public image the white man has fashioned to characterize Black Men are references by Black Men to the identity of Black Men in the West, since that's what is run on them each day by white magic, *i.e.*, television, movies, radio, etc.—the Mass Media (the *Daily News* does it with flicks and adjectives).

The song title "A White Man's Heaven Is a Black Man's Hell" describes how complete an image reversal is necessary in the West. Because for many Black People, the white man has succeeded in making this hell seem like heaven. But Black youth are much better off in this regard than their parents. They are the ones who need the least image reversal.

The Black artist, in this context, is desperately needed to change the images his people identify with, by asserting Black feeling, Black mind, Black judgment. The Black intellectual, in this same context, is needed to change the interpretation of facts toward the Black

Man's best interests, instead of merely tagging along reciting white judgments of the world.

Art, Religion, and Politics are impressive vectors of a culture. Art describes a culture. Black artists must have an image of what the Black sensibility is in this land. Religion elevates a culture. The Black Man must aspire to Blackness. God is man idealized. The Black Man must idealize himself as Black. And idealize and aspire to that. Politics gives a social order to the culture, *i.e.*, makes relationships within the culture definable for the functioning organism. The Black man must seek a Black politics, an ordering of the world that is beneficial to his culture, to his interiorization and judgment of the world. This is strength. And we are hordes.

4

Black People are a race, a culture, a Nation. The legacy of Malcolm X is that we know we can move from where we are. Our land is where we live. (Even the Muslims have made this statement about Harlem.) If we are a separate Nation, we must make that separateness where we are. There are Black cities all over this white nation. Nations within nations. In order for the Black Man to survive he must not only identify himself as a unique being, but take steps to insure that this being has what the Germans call *Lebensraum* ("living room"), literally space in which to exist and develop.

The concepts of National Consciousness and the Black Nation, after the death of Malik, have moved to the point where now some Black People are demanding national sovereignty as well as National (and Cultural) Consciousness. In Harlem, for instance, as director of the Black Arts Repertory Theatre School, I have issued a call for a Black Nation. In Harlem, where 600,000 Black People reside.

The first act must be the nationalization of all properties and resources belonging to white people, within the boundaries of the Black Nation. (All the large concentrations of Black People in the West are already nations. All that is missing is the consciousness of this state of affairs. All that is missing is that the Black Man take control. As Margaret Walker said in her poem "For My People": *A race of men must rise, and take control*.)

Nationalization means that all properties and resources must be harnessed to the needs of the Nation. In the case of the coming Black Nation, all these materials must be harnessed to the needs of Black People. In Harlem, it is almost common knowledge that the Jews, etc., will go the next time there's a large "disturbance," like they say. But there must be machinery set up to transfer the power potential of these retail businesses, small industries, etc., so that they may benefit Black People.

Along with nationalization of foreign-owned businesses (which includes Italian underworld businesses, some of which, like the policy racket, can be transformed into a national lottery, with the monies staying with Black People, or as in the case of heroin-selling, completely abolished) must come the nationalization of all political voices setting up to function within the community/Nation.

No white politicians can be allowed to function within the Nation. Black politicians doing funny servant business for whites must be eliminated. Black people must have absolute political and economic control. In other words they must have absolute control over their lives and destinies.

These moves are toward the working form of any autonomous nation. And it is this that the Black Man must have. An autonomous Nation. His own forms: treaties, agreements, laws.

These are moves that the conscious Black Man (artist, intellectual, Nationalist, religious thinker, dude with "common sense") must prepare the people for. And the people must be prepared for moves they themselves are already making. And moves they have already made must be explained and analyzed. They, the people, are the bodies . . . Where are the heads?

And it is *the heads* that are needed for the next move Black People will make. The move to Nationhood. The exact method of transformation is simple logistics.

What we are speaking about again is sovereignty. Sovereignty and independence. And when we speak of these things, we can understand just how far Malik went. The point now is to take ourselves the rest of the way.

Only a united Black Consciousness can save Black People from annihilation at the white man's hands. And no other nation on earth is safe, unless the Black Man in America is safe. Not even the Chinese can be absolutely certain of their continued sovereignty as long as the white man is alive. And there is only one people on the planet who can slay the white man. The people who know him best. His ex-slaves.

state/meant

The Black Artist's role in America is to aid in the destruction of America as he knows it. His role is to report and reflect so precisely the nature of the society, and of himself in that society, that other men will be moved by the exactness of his rendering and, if they are black men, grow strong through this moving, having seen their own strength, and weakness; and if they are white men, tremble, curse, and go mad, because they will be drenched with the filth of their evil.

The Black Artist must draw out of his soul the correct image of the world. He must use this image to band his brothers and sisters together in common understanding of the nature of the world (and the nature of America) and the nature of the human soul.

The Black Artist must demonstrate sweet life, how it differs from the deathly grip of the White Eyes. The Black Artist must teach the White Eyes their deaths, and teach the black man how to bring these deaths about.

> We are unfair, and unfair.
> We are black magicians, black art
> s we make in black labs of the heart.

> The fair are
> fair, and death
> ly white.

The day will not save them
and we own
the night.

Also available from Akashic Books

TALES OF THE OUT & THE GONE
short stories by Amiri Baraka
224 pages, trade paperback original, $14.95
*Winner of a 2008 PEN/Beyond Margins Award

"As this new collection of short fiction (most of it previously unpublished) makes clear, the writer formerly known as LeRoi Jones possesses an outtelligence of a high order. Baraka is such a provocateur, so skilled at prodding his perceived enemies in their tender underbellies, that it becomes easy to overlook that he is first and foremost a writer . . . He writes crisp, punchy sentences and has a fine ear for dialogue . . . In his prose as in his poetry, Baraka is at his best as a lyrical prophet of despair who transfigures his contentious racial and political views into a transcendent, 'outtelligent' clarity."
—*New York Times Book Review* (Editors' Choice)

THE HUNGERED ONE
short stories by Ed Bullins (with a Preface by Amiri Baraka)
192 pages, trade paperback, $14.95

"A richness of language and observation pervades this collection of short stories by a black writer about real black people."
—*New York Times Book Review*

"There are master works here . . . But there is also an edgy silent harshness, a world held together by yearning and regret, where desire is met with smothered instinct, hope with mocking laughter . . . However bitter, it's good for us."
—Amiri Baraka, from the Preface

THE AGE OF DREAMING
a novel by Nina Revoyr
330 pages, trade paperback original, $15.95

"Fast-moving, riveting, unpredictable, and profound; highly recommended for all fiction collections."
—*Library Journal*

"Few subjects generate clichés more readily than Hollywood, yet Revoyr has steered clear of every stereotype while perfectly capturing the promise of classic movie-star dreams . . . Rare indeed is a novel this deeply pleasurable and significant."
—*Booklist* (starred review)

SONG FOR NIGHT
a novella by Chris Abani
168 pages, trade paperback original, $12.95
*Winner of a 2008 PEN/Beyond Margins Award

"*Song for Night* contains, at once, an extraordinary ferocity and a vulnerable beauty all its own."
—*New York Times Book Review* (Editors' Choice)

"What makes this book a luminous addition to the burgeoning literature on boy soldiers is the way the Nigerian author both undercuts and reinforces such hopeful sentiments . . . The lyrical intensity of the writing perfectly suits the material."
—*Los Angeles Times Book Review*

SOUTH BY SOUTH BRONX
a novel by Abraham Rodriguez
292 pages, trade paperback original, $15.95

"More than a crime tale, this is also a gritty exploration of love and art."
—*Library Journal*

"The novel takes the Bronx-born writer's longtime concerns about Puerto Rican identity and street-level realism and meshes them with the structure of a classic pulp fiction narrative."
—*New York Daily News*

LIKE SON
a novel by Felicia Luna Lemus
266 pages, trade paperback original, $14.95

"Lemus introduces a compelling protagonist whose explorations of passion, death, and memory combine with contemporary societal urgencies to tell an ancient story about love that's worth waiting for."
—*Out*